Python®
Create-Modify-Reuse

Python®
Create-Modify-Reuse

Jim Knowlton

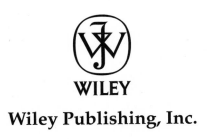

WILEY

Wiley Publishing, Inc.

Python® : Create-Modify-Reuse

Published by
Wiley Publishing, Inc.
10475 Crosspoint Boulevard
Indianapolis, IN 46256
www.wiley.com

Published simultaneously in Canada

ISBN: 978-0-470-25932-0

Manufactured in the United States of America

10 9 8 7 6 5 4 3 2 1

Library of Congress Cataloging-in-Publication Data

Knowlton, Jim.
    Python : create-modify-reuse / Jim Knowlton.
      p. cm.
    Includes index.
    ISBN 978-0-470-25932-0 (paper/website)
      1. Python (Computer program language)   I. Title.
  QA76.73.P98K56   2008
  005.13'3—dc22

                    2008021374

To Karin, the love of my life. Words simply can't express all that I'm grateful for. I know that sometimes I live in another world — but always know that it would be a cold world without you.

To my children, Karren, Shannon, Kasey, Brian, Courtney, Jaren, Carlen, Kristin, Logan, and Ben — and to little Olivia yet to come (as I write this). For some of you I was there at your birth, some of you I have known for only a few years, but know that each one of you is a treasure to me.

To Mom and Dad, you are still with me every day. I live to make you proud.

About the Author

Jim Knowlton is a software quality engineer with Automatic Data Processing (ADP), Inc., where he leads quality assurance efforts on ADP's computer telephony integration and network video projects. He has been instrumental in introducing automated testing methodologies to their QA effort. He has more than fifteen years of experience in the software industry, including clients such as Symantec, Novell, Nike, and Zions Bank. He has extensive experience in open-source technologies, including Python, Ruby, PHP, Apache, and MySQL, and has also worked extensively in the areas of systems management and enterprise security. Jim holds a bachelor of arts degree in management and is currently working on a master of software engineering degree at Portland State University.

Credits

Acquisitions Editor
Jenny Watson

Development Editor
Ed Connor

Technical Editor
Jesse Keating

Production Editor
Daniel Scribner

Copy Editor
Expat Editing

Editorial Manager
Mary Beth Wakefield

Production Manager
Tim Tate

Vice President and Executive Group Publisher
Richard Swadley

Vice President and Executive Publisher
Joseph B. Wikert

Project Coordinator, Cover
Lynsey Stanford

Proofreader
Nancy Carrasco

Indexer
Robert Swanson

Acknowledgments

First, I'd like to acknowledge Guido Van Rossum for creating such a way cool language as Python.

I'd like to thank my agent, Neil Salkind, for nursing my insecurities and answering my novice writer questions.

I'd like to thank Jenny Watson, my acquisitions editor at Wiley, for being willing to go to bat for an unpublished writer's crazy ideas. Thanks to Ed Connor, my development editor, for his gentle prodding, high standards, and encouragement. Thanks also to Jesse Keating for his help with technical editing, and to Brent Rufener for providing a cover photo.

Finally, but most important, thanks to my family for putting up with my frequent unavailability during the last few months — writing is a solitary art, and it will be nice to reacquaint myself with my loved ones.

Contents

Contents

Contents

Contents

Introduction

Python: Create-Modify-Reuse is designed for all levels of Python developers interested in a practical, hands-on way of learning Python development. This book is designed to show you how to use Python (in combination with the raw processing power of your computer) to accomplish real-world tasks in a more efficient way. Don't look for an exhaustive description of the Python language — you won't find it. The book's main purpose is not to thoroughly cover the Python language, but rather to show how you can use Python to create robust, real-world applications.

In this respect, the goal is similar to foreign-language books that identify themselves as "conversational," focusing on the vocabulary and concepts that people will need the most. Likewise, I focus specifically on the Python knowledge needed to accomplish practical, specific tasks. Along the way, you will learn to create useful, efficient scripts that are easy to maintain and enhance.

The applications, along with source code, are available for download at www.wrox.com.

Who This Book Is For

This book is for developers with some experience with Python who want to explore how to develop full-blown applications. It is also for developers with experience in other languages who want to learn Python by building robust applications. It is well-suited for developers who like to "learn by doing," rather than exploring a language feature by feature. To get the most out of the book, you should understand basic programming principles.

Because this book is project-based, you can approach it in numerous ways. You can, of course, read it from cover to cover. Chapters 2 through 8 each cover a different project, so the chapters are independent of each other. However, because each chapter project is covered individually, there may be some overlap of information. I also sometimes refer to explanations of particular topics covered in previous chapters. This will help to reinforce important concepts.

The end of the book contains two appendixes. The first one is a listing of Python resources you can check out for more information. The second one will help you with installing additional components used in some of the examples.

What This Book Covers

I've always liked the Saturday morning fix-it shows that demonstrate how to build something, such as a cabinet or a deck. The experts on these shows take seemingly large, complex tasks that appear to be beyond the skill level of the average do-it-yourselfer and break them down into smaller, simple tasks, teaching you valuable skills along the way. That's basically the intention and approach taken in this book, applied to the construction of software instead of home improvements.

This book starts with a basic overview of the Python language, designed for those familiar with other languages but new to Python. It is followed by several chapters, each of which describes a complete project that can be used as-is or modified and extended to suit your particular purposes. You'll find applications that access databases, take advantage of web technologies, and facilitate network communications, to name a few. In addition, and more important than the technologies you will be introduced to, you will learn how to use Python to solve real challenges. Following these chapters are two chapters that cover accessing operating system resources and debugging and testing, respectively.

Each project chapter contains complete instructions describing how to install and use the application, so you can actually see the program run as you learn how to construct and use it, including how the project was designed and prototyped. This book is intended to be both a reference guide and a learning aid, teaching you how to build solutions with Python and providing reference information on a wide variety of Python programming concepts.

It is hoped that this book will help you have fun with Python and build useful applications, and — unlike my experience with building a deck — without sore thumbs.

How This Book Is Structured

This book is framed around the code itself. This is because developers are typically looking for how to do something; and, as with many activities, you learn how to do something by watching how others do it and trying it yourself. If you want to know how a `for` loop works, you'll find `for` loops in my code, but that's not the thrust of the book. Instead, this book shows you how to do things: how to build a content management system, how to build a test management system, how to set up a system for tracking customer follow-up, and so on. Along the way, you'll learn how to communicate with a SQL database, how to act as a web server or communicate with one, how to access operating system services, and more.

There are three basic components to the book:

❑   Chapter 1 is a brief overview of the Python language.

❑   Chapters 2–8 cover seven different programming projects, which illustrate various technologies and techniques available to Python developers.

❑   Chapters 9–10 cover additional, advanced topics, which will help you as you build Python projects.

The project chapters have a consistent structure:

- ❑ Overview: What does the application do?
- ❑ Using the program
- ❑ Design
    - ❑ How it all fits together
    - ❑ Modules involved
- ❑ Code and code explanation
    - ❑ Module/class 1 explanation
    - ❑ Module/class 2 explanation
    - ❑ Minor code file explanation
- ❑ Testing, including suggested tests
- ❑ Modifying the project, including some suggested adaptations
- ❑ Summary

Each project is designed with classes that can be reused and accessed for multiple purposes. This is one of the main benefits of object-oriented programming, so designing for reusability is a main focus of the book. The book contains the following chapters:

1. A Python Primer

This chapter is a basic primer on the Python language, and it functions as either a quick tutorial for experienced programmers new to Python or a refresher for programmers with Python experience.

Part I: The Projects

2. Directory/File Snapshot Program

This project demonstrates how to interact with files, create and manipulate data structures, and provide user output. It also touches on code design issues to improve code maintainability. Often when installing or uninstalling software, or verifying changes to a file system, it can be valuable to take a "snapshot" of the files and directories, along with their size and last-modified time. The script introduced in this chapter does just that. This chapter also explores how to capture a directory listing into a Python list, and explains how to query this list for particular values.

3. DVD Inventory System

This project takes advantage of Python's capability to access and manipulate data in a SQL database. The application enables multiple users to log in to a website that provides access to a DVD inventory database. Permissions are set such that some users can add, modify, or delete entries, whereas other users have read-only access to the data.

4. Web Performance Tester

This project shows how to communicate with a Python web server and retrieve information regarding how long it takes to receive requested items from the web server. Although writing Python programs to work on a single computer can be useful, the real power of Python can be seen when it is used to script communication between computers on a network. Most networks contain several web servers. A nice feature of Python is that it can act as a lightweight server for various Internet protocols, such as HTTP (web) and ftp. This application enables you to monitor performance of HTTP traffic on your network.

5. Customer Follow-Up System

This project shows how to present a web form to the user and retrieve data from it, how to automatically format and send e-mail through an SMTP server, and how to generate an HTML-formatted report. The task for the second example is to automatically generate a customer comments e-mail message based on information the customer enters in a form. It uses the mod_python Apache module to take the information entered in the HTTP form and then utilizes a Python script on the web server to send that information to an SMTP server for mail delivery.

6. Test Management/Reporting System

This project makes use of the unittest module to run tests against an existing application, and creates a framework for reporting test results. Testing is a vital process for developing software. This application enables users to run tests for a given piece of software, to list the previous test runs by date, to show test run results for any previously run tests, and to output the results of any test run as HTML for viewing in a web browser.

7. Version Management System

This project connects to a list of servers via telnet, checks the application version of a pre-set application list, and displays its results both as output and to a log file. Often, a system administrator needs to patch systems or ensure that systems have the latest application versions installed. This script is an easy way to accomplish that task. It makes use of Python's capability to emulate a telnet client and log in to remote systems and perform functions on that remote system.

8. Content Management System

This project explores Plone, a popular content management system based on Python and Zope (a Python-based application server). Because Python is a very mature language, numerous applications have been built on top of it. A great thing about working with Python-based applications is that you get the benefit of a full-blown application, but you can still use Python to configure and customize it.

Part II: Advanced Topics

9. Interacting with the Operating System

When writing scripts "in the real world," often it is critical to be able to access services available through (and particular to) the operating system you happen to be on. For example, suppose you wanted to read or modify the Window Registry? Or you wanted to get the Linux process ID of a particular process that is running? Is such a thing even possible? Definitely — and this chapter shows you how.

10. Debugging and Testing

Because I am a software tester myself, testing is a subject that is certainly close to my heart. In this chapter, I discuss why testing is important, how to put the right amount of testing into your code, and how writing automated tests can help you to actually write code more quickly. You'll look at PyUnit, the automated testing framework for Python, and learn how to use it to test the riskiest parts of a script. You'll also explore the Python debugger and some of the nifty features it offers.

Appendix A   Where to Go from Here: Resources That Can Help

This appendix provides an annotated list of books, websites, and blogs that can provide useful information, insight, and inspiration for the budding Python script developer.

Appendix B   Installing Supplemental Programs

This appendix provides detailed information on how to set up MySQL (used in the project in Chapter 3) and PyWin32 (used in Chapter 10 and various other projects in the book).

What You Need to Use This Book

For this book, I used Python 2.51 (the "CPython" distribution), run on Windows, as my Python distribution of choice. Most of the examples will work with the latest versions of Python for Windows, Mac, or Unix/Linux, or IronPython. However, to successfully run everything in this book, you'll want the latest version of CPython on Windows, which is currently version 2.51.

Other applications, such as Plone, are available free and can be downloaded as needed. When you get to a chapter for which you need an additional component, I'll indicate that to you, and you can look in Appendix B for information on installing additional components.

Source Code

As you work through the examples in this book, you may choose either to type in all the code manually or to use the source code files that accompany the book. All of the source code used in this book is available for download at www.wrox.com. Once at the site, simply locate the book's title (either by using the Search box or by using one of the title lists) and click the Download Code link on the book's detail page to obtain all the source code for the book.

> **Because many books have similar titles, you may find it easiest to search by ISBN; this book's ISBN is 978-0-470-25932-0.**

Once you download the code, just decompress it with your favorite compression tool. Alternately, you can go to the main Wrox code download page at www.wrox.com/dynamic/books/download.aspx to see the code available for this book and all other Wrox books.

Errata

We make every effort to ensure that there are no errors in the text or in the code. However, no one is perfect and mistakes do occur. If you find an error in one of our books, such as a spelling mistake or faulty piece of code, we would be very grateful for your feedback. By sending in errata you may save another reader hours of frustration and at the same time you will be helping us provide even higher quality information.

To find the errata page for this book, go to www.wrox.com and locate the title using the Search box or one of the title lists. Then, on the book details page, click the Book Errata link. On this page you can view all errata that has been submitted for this book and posted by Wrox editors. A complete book list including links to each book's errata is also available at www.wrox.com/misc-pages/booklist.shtml.

If you don't spot "your" error on the Book Errata page, go to www.wrox.com/contact/techsupport .shtml and complete the form there to send us the error you have found. I'll check the information and, if appropriate, post a message to the book's errata page and fix the problem in subsequent editions of the book.

p2p.wrox.com

For author and peer discussion, join the P2P forums at p2p.wrox.com. The forums are a Web-based system for you to post messages relating to Wrox books and related technologies and interact with other readers and technology users. The forums offer a subscription feature to e-mail you topics of interest of your choosing when new posts are made to the forums. Wrox authors, editors, other industry experts, and your fellow readers are present on these forums.

At http://p2p.wrox.com you will find a number of different forums that will help you not only as you read this book, but also as you develop your own applications. To join the forums, just follow these steps:

1. Go to p2p.wrox.com and click the Register link.
2. Read the terms of use and click Agree.

3. Complete the required information to join, as well as any optional information you wish to provide and click Submit.

4. You will receive an e-mail with information describing how to verify your account and complete the joining process.

> **You can read messages in the forums without joining P2P but in order to post your own messages, you must join.**

Once you join, you can post new messages and respond to messages other users post. You can read messages at any time on the Web. If you would like to have new messages from a particular forum e-mailed to you, click the Subscribe to this Forum icon by the forum name in the forum listing.

For more information about how to use the Wrox P2P, be sure to read the P2P FAQs for answers to questions about how the forum software works, as well as many common questions specific to P2P and Wrox books. To read the FAQs, click the FAQ link on any P2P page.

1

A Python Primer

This chapter provides a quick overview of the Python language. The goal in this chapter is not to teach you the Python language — excellent books have been written on that subject, such as *Beginning Python* (Wrox, 2005). This chapter describes Python's lexical structure and programming conventions, so if you are familiar with other scripting languages such as Perl or Ruby, or with compiled programming languages such as Java or C#, you should easily be up to speed in no time.

Getting Started

Of course, the first thing you need to do is install Python, if you don't already have it. Installers are available for Windows, Macintosh, Linux, Unix, and everything from OpenVMS to the Playstation (no, I'm not kidding).

Obtaining Python and Installing It

If you go to `www.python.org/download` you can find links to download the correct version of Python for your operating system. Follow the install instructions for your particular Python distribution — instructions can vary significantly depending on what operating system you're installing to.

> ### What Version Number to Install
>
> Although the examples in this book should work for any Python version above 2.0, it is best to install the latest stable build for your operating system. For Windows (which is the environment I primarily work in), the latest stable version is 2.51. There is an alpha build of Python 3.0 available as of this writing, but other than just looking at it for fun, I'd steer clear of it for the examples in this book — in some cases the syntax is very different, and the examples in this book won't work with Python 3.0.

The Python Interpreter

One of the most useful tools for writing Python code is the *Python interpreter*, an interactive editing and execution environment in which commands are run as soon as you enter them and press Enter. On Unix and Macintosh machines, the Python interpreter can usually be found in the `/usr/local/bin/python` directory, which can be accessed by simply typing the command **python**.

On Windows machines, the Python interpreter is installed to the `c:\python25` directory (for a Python 2.5x installation). To add this directory to your path, type the following at a Windows command prompt: **set path=%path%;C:\python25.**

On a Windows system, such as with Unix/Linux, you simply type **python** to bring up the interpreter (either from the `c:\python25` directory or from any directory if the Python directory has been added to the path).

When you enter the interpreter, you'll see a screen with information like the following:

```
Python 2.5.1 (r251:54863, Apr 18 2007, 08:51:08) [MSC v.1310 32 bit (Intel)] on win32
Type "help", "copyright", "credits" or "license" for more information.
>>>
```

Your Editing/Execution Environment

Because the minimum requirements for writing and running Python programs are simply an editor that can save text files and a command prompt where you can run the Python interpreter, you could simply use Notepad on Windows, Vim on Linux/Unix, or TextEdit on Mac, and a command line for running programs.

One nice step up from that is IDLE, Python's integrated development environment (IDE), which is named after Monty Python's Eric Idle and is included with Python. It includes the following useful features:

- ❏ A full-featured text editor
- ❏ Syntax highlighting
- ❏ Code intelligence
- ❏ A class browser
- ❏ A Python path browser
- ❏ A debugger
- ❏ A Python interpreter environment

In addition to IDLE, you do have other options. On Windows, there is a nice IDE called PythonWin, developed by Mark Hammond. It can be installed as a full Python distribution from ActiveState's website (`www.activestate.com`), or you can simply install the win32all package to add PythonWin to a standard Python for Windows install. PythonWin is a great product, very slick and with all the features you'd expect from an IDE.

Other options include an Eclipse distribution for Python called EasyEclipse for Python. For my money, I'd start out with IDLE, and then as your experience with Python grows, explore other options.

Lexical Structure

Following is a simple Python program. It shows the basic structure of many Python scripts, which is as follows:

1. Initialize variables (lines 1–3).

2. Do some processing (lines 4–5).

3. Make decisions and perform actions based on those decisions (lines 6–10).

```python
name = "Jim"
age = 42
highschoolGPA = 3.89

enteredName = raw_input("Enter your name: ")

print "\n\n"

if name == "Jim":
    print "Your age is ", age
    print "You had a", highschoolGPA, "GPA in high school"
    if (highschoolGPA > 3):
        print "You had better than a 3.0 GPA...good job!"
```

Keywords

Keywords are words that are "reserved" — they cannot be used as variable names. In the preceding code, the keyword `if` is used multiple times.

The keywords are as follows:

and	del	for	is	raise
assert	elif	from	lambda	return
break	else	global	not	try
class	except	if	or	while
continue	exec	import	pass	
def	finally	in	print	yield

Lines and Indentation

In Python, unlike a compiled language such as C, line breaks are significant, and the end of a program statement is defined by a hard return. Program blocks are defined by a combination of statements (each on a separate line, but with no end-of-statement character visible) and program blocks, delimited visually by the use of indentation.

As shown in the code from the preceding section, lines are indented in Python. This is not simply a stylistic choice — indentation is not just recommended in Python, but enforced by the interpreter. This is probably the most controversial aspect of Python, and it has been the subject of many a flame war online.

Basically, it means that the following code would generate an interpreter error, because the action associated with an `if` statement must be indented:

```
if variable1 == "Jim":
print "variable1 eqiuals Jim"
```

You'll learn more about the actual `if` statement itself later.

Data Types and Identifiers

Python provides a rich collection of data types to enable programmers to perform virtually any programming task they desire in another language. One nice thing about Python is that it provides many useful and unique data types (such as tuples and dictionaries), and stays away from data types such as the pointers used in C, which have their use but can also make programming much more confusing and difficult for the nonprofessional programmer.

Data Types

Python is known as a *dynamically typed* language, which means that you don't have to explicitly identify the data type when you initialize a variable. In the code example above, the variable `name` is assigned to the string value "Jim". However, you don't specifically identify the variable as a string variable. Python knows, based on the value it has been given, that it should allocate memory for a string. Likewise for the `age` integer variable and the `highschoolGPA` float variable.

The following table shows the most commonly used available data types and their attributes:

Data Type	Attributes	Example
Numeric Types		
Float	Implemented with C doubles.	5.43 9483.123
Integer	Implemented with C longs.	1027 211234
Long Integer	Size is limited only by system resources.	567893L
Sequence Types		
String	A list of characters. Is immutable (not changeable in-place). Can be represented by single quotes or double quotes. Can span multiple lines.	"This is a string" """ This is an example of a DocString """
List	A mutable (changeable) sequence of data types. List elements do not have to be "like." In other words, you could have a float element and an integer element in a single list.	[1, 2.3, "Jim"] [1, 2, 3] [1.5, 2.7, 3.0] ["Jim", "Joe", "Bob"]
Tuple	An immutable sequence of data types. Other than the fact that it can't be changed, it works just like a list.	(1, 2.3, "Jim") (1, 2, 3) (1.5, 2.7, 3.0) "Jim", "Joe", "Bob"
Dictionary	A list of items indexed by keys.	d = {"first":"Jim", "last":"Knowlton"}

Identifiers

An *identifier* is a unique name that enables you to identify something. Identifiers are used to label variables, functions, classes, objects, and modules. They begin with either a letter or an underscore, and they can contain letters, underscores, or digits. They cannot contain punctuation marks.

Operators

If you have programmed in other languages, the operators in Python will be familiar to you. The Python operators are fundamentally similar to those used in other languages. In the code shown earlier, the conditions evaluated in both `if` statements involve comparison operators. The following table describes the operators most commonly used in Python, and the ones used in this book:

Operator	Symbol	Example
Numeric Operators		
Addition	+	x + y
Subtraction	–	x – y
Multiplication	*	x * y
Division	/	x / y
Exponent (Power)	**	x ** y (x to the y power)
Modulo	%	x % y (the remainder of x/y)
Comparison Operators		
Greater than	>	x > y (x is greater than y)
Less than	<	x < y (x is less than y)
Equal to	==	x == y (x equals y)
Greater than or equal to	>=	x >= y (x is greater than or equal to y)
Less than or equal to	<=	x <= y (x is less than or equal to y)
Not equal to	!= or <>	x != y, x <> y (x does not equal y)
Boolean Operators		
and	and	x and y (if both are true, then the expression is true)
or	or	x or y (if either is true, then the expression is true)
not	not	not x (if x is false, then the expression is true)
Assignment Operator		
Assignment	=	X = 15 name = "Jim"

Expressions and Statements

Expressions and statements are the building blocks of Python programs. They are the equivalent of phrases and sentences in English. To understand Python, it's critical to understand how to put these building blocks together.

Expressions

Expressions consist of combinations of *values*, which can be either constant values, such as a string ("Jim") or a number (12), and *operators*, which are symbols that act on the values in some way.

The following examples are expressions:

```
10 - 4

11 * (4 + 5)

x - 5

a / b
```

Operator Precedence in Expressions

When you have a multiple expression like `5 + 4 * 7`, which operation is done first, the addition or the multiplication? If it isn't too painful to recall your high school algebra class, you might remember learning the rules of *operator precedence*. These kinds of complex expressions require a set of rules defining which expressions are executed first.

The following list describes the basic rules of operator precedence in Python (don't worry if you don't understand all the terms right now; they'll be explained as you need them):

❏ Expressions are evaluated from left to right.

❏ Exponents, multiplication, and division are performed before addition and subtraction.

❏ Expressions in parentheses are performed first.

❏ Mathematical expressions are performed before Boolean expressions (AND, OR, NOT).

Statements

The *statement* is the basic unit of programming. In essence, it says "do this to this." Statements in Python are not delimited by a visible character, such as the semicolon in C or C#. Every time you press Enter and start a new line, you are entering a new statement.

For example, if you type:

```
Print 12 + 15
```

into the Python interpreter, you'll get the following output:

```
>>> print 12 + 15
27
>>>
```

This is because you told the system to "print the result of the expression 12 + 15," which is a complete statement.

However, if you type:

```
print 12 +
```

you'll get a syntax error, as shown here:

```
>>> print 12 +
SyntaxError: invalid syntax
>>>
```

Clearly, the system cannot read this because it isn't a complete statement, so it results in an error.

Multi-line Statements

It *is* possible to have a single statement span multiple lines. You could do this for aesthetic reasons or simply because the line is too long to read on one screen. To do this, simply put a space and a backslash at the end of the line. Here are a few examples:

```
name = "Jim \
    Knowlton"

sum = 12 + \
    13
```

Iteration and Decision-Making

There are two basic ways to control the flow of a program: through iteration (looping) and through decision-making.

Iteration

Iteration in Python is handled through the "usual suspects": the `for` loop and the `while` loop. However, if you've programmed in other languages, these seemingly familiar friends are a little different.

For Loops

Unlike in Java, the `for` loop in Python is more than a simple construct based on a counter. Instead, it is a sequence iterator that will step through the items of any sequenced object (such as a list of names, for instance). Here's a simple example of a `for` loop:

```
>>> names = ["Jim", "Joe"]
>>> for x in names:
  print x


  Jim
  Joe
>>>
```

As you can see, the basic syntax is `for <variable> in <object>:`, followed by the code block to be iterated.

While Loops

A `while` loop is similar to a `for` loop but it's more flexible. It enables you to test for a particular condition and then terminate the loop when the condition is true. This is great for situations when you want to terminate a loop when the program is in a state that you can't predict at runtime (such as when you are processing a file, and you want the loop to be done when you reach the end of the file).

Here's an example of a `while` loop:

```
>>> counter = 5
>>> x = 0
>>> while x < counter:
  print "x=",x
  print "counter = ", counter
  x += 1


x =  0
counter =  5
x =  1
counter =  5
x =  2
counter =  5
x =  3
counter =  5
x =  4
counter =  5
>>>
```

9

Break and Continue

As with C, in Python you can break out of the innermost `for` or `while` loop by using the `break` statement. Also as with C, you can continue to the next iteration of a loop by using the `continue` statement.

What about switch or case?

Many of you familiar with other programming languages are no doubt wondering about a decision-tree structure similar to C's switch statement or Pascal's case. Unfortunately, you won't find it in Python. However, the conditional `if-elif-else` structure, along with other constructs you'll learn about later, make their absence not such a big deal.

Decision-Making

When writing a program, it is of course critical to be able to evaluate conditions and make decisions. Having an `if` construct is critical for any language, and Python is no exception.

The if Statement

The `if` statement in Python, as in other languages, evaluates an expression. If the expression is true, then the code block is executed. Conversely, if it isn't true, then program execution jumps to the end. Python also supports use of zero or more `elif` statements (short for "else if"), and an optional `else` statement, which appears at the end if you also have `elif` statements, and would be the "default" choice if none of the `if` statements were true.

Here's an example:

```
>>> name = "Jim"
>>> if name == "Jim":
 print "your name is Jim"
elif name == "Joe":
 print "your name is Joe"
else:
 print "I have no idea what your name is"


your name is Jim
>>>
```

Functions

In many ways, the principle behind a function is analogous to turning on a TV. You don't have to understand all the electronics and communications technology behind getting the TV signal to your receiver in order to operate the TV. You do have to know some simple behaviors, however, such as how to turn it on, where the volume switch is, and so on. In a similar fashion, a function gives the program an interface through which it can run program code without knowing the details about the code being run.

Defining a Function

You define a function in Python with the following simple syntax:

```
def functionName(paramenter1, parameter2=default_value):
 <code block>
 return value (optional)
```

Note two elements in the preceding example:

❑ **Parameters** — As you can see, parameters can simply be a variable name (making them required as part of the function call), or they can have a default value, in which case it is optional to pass them in the function call.

❑ **The return statement** — This enables the function to return a value to the code that called it. The nice thing about this is that you can run a function and assign its output to a variable.

Here's an example of a function definition:

```
>>> def getname(name):
 return name + " is very hungry"

>>>
```

Calling a Function

To call a function, simply enter the function name with the function signature:

```
functionName(paramenter1, parameter2)
```

If a parameter has a default value in its definition, then you can omit that parameter when you call the function, and the parameter will contain its default value. Alternately, you can override the default value by entering the value yourself when you call the function.

For example, if a function were defined as follows:

```
def jimsFunc(age, name = "Jim"):
```

Then you could call the function in any of the following three ways:

```
jimsFunc(23)

jimsFunc(42, "James")
jimsFunc(42, firstName="Joe")
```

In the first example, I simply took the default value for the first parameter; in the second, I replaced it with "James."

Modules

A *module* is the highest-level programming unit in Python. A module usually corresponds to a program file in Python. Unlike in Ruby, modules are not declared — the name of the *.py file is the name of the module. In other words, basically each file is a module, and modules import other modules to perform various programming tasks.

Importing Modules

Importing modules is done with either the import or reload command.

Import

To use a module, you import it. Usually import statements occur at the beginning of the Python module. Importing modules is a fairly simple operation, but it requires a little explanation. Consider the following examples:

```
1.      import os
2.      import os, sys
3.      from os import getcwd
4.      import os as operatingSystem
```

These examples highlight some variations in how you can import modules:

1. This first example is the simplest and easiest to understand. It is merely the keyword import followed by the module name (in this case, os).

2. Multiple modules can be imported with the same import command, with the modules separated by a comma.

3. You can import specific names only within a module, without importing the whole module, by using the `from <module> import <name>` statement. This can be useful for performance reasons if you only need one function from a large module.

4. If a module has a name that's difficult to work with or remember, and you want to use a name to represent it that is meaningful to you, simply use the `as` keyword and `import <module> as <identifier>`.

Reload

`Reload` is another very useful command, especially when entering code within the Python interactive interpreter. It enables you to reload a particular module without reloading Python. For example, if you wanted to reload the `os` module, you would simply enter `reload os`.

If you're wondering why you would ever want to do that, one scenario would be if you have a Python script that runs all the time and it accesses a module on another machine. Assuming you always want to ensure that you're running the most current version of the remote module you're accessing, you'd use the `reload` command.

How Python Finds Modules to Load

When you use an `import` statement, you don't tell Python where the module that needs to be loaded is located. How, then, does it know where to find the file? The answer to that question is the *module search path*.

The Module Search Path

Python has a predefined priority specifying where it should look for modules, known as the module search path. When you enter an `import` command and the name of the module, Python checks the following locations in the order shown here:

1. **The home directory** — This is either the directory from which you launched the Python interactive interpreter or the directory where the main Python program is located.

2. `PYTHONPATH` — This is an environment variable set in the system. Its value is a list of directories, which Python will search for modules.

3. **Standard library directories** — The directory in which the standard libraries are located are searched next.

Exploring sys.path

If you ever want to see your system's Python search path, all you have to do is bring up the interactive interpreter, import the `sys` module, and type **sys.path**. The full Python module search path will be returned, as shown in the following example:

```
>>> import sys
>>> sys.path
['C:\\Python25', 'C:\\Python25\\Lib\\idlelib', 'C:\\Program Files\\PythonNet',
'c:\\scripts\\python', 'c:\\python25', 'C:\\Python25\\pyunit-1.4.1',
'c:\\python25\\pamie', 'C:\\WINDOWS\\system32\\python25.zip', 'C:\\Python25\\DLLs',
'C:\\Python25\\lib', 'C:\\Python25\\lib\\plat-win', 'C:\\Python25\\lib\\lib-tk',
'C:\\Python25\\lib\\site-packages', 'C:\\Python25\\lib\\site-packages\\win32',
'C:\\Python25\\lib\\site-packages\\win32\\lib', 'C:\\Python25\\lib\\site-
packages\\
Pythonwin', 'C:\\Python25\\lib\\site-packages\\wx-2.8-msw-ansi']
>>>
```

Classes

Python is a language that can support both procedural programming and object-oriented programming. Here is an example of a Python class:

```
>>> class name1():
 def setmyname(self, myname):
        self.name = myname


>>> jimname = name1()
>>> jimname.setmyname("Jim")
>>> print jimname.name
Jim
>>>
```

Note some points about Python's implementation of class programming as demonstrated in the preceding example:

❑ If we were inheriting from other classes, those class names would have been inside the parentheses of the `class name1():` definition.

❑ In this case, there is one class method, `setmyname`. If we wanted to create a constructor for the class, it would be named `__init__`.

❑ To create an instance of a class, you simply assign a variable to the class definition, as in `jimname = name1()`.

❑ Attributes are accessed with familiar dot notation (instance `variable.attribute`) such as `jimname.name`.

Summary

This chapter provided a brief tour of the Python language, including the following highlights:

- ❑   How to get up and running with Python
- ❑   Python's lexical structure
- ❑   Operators, expressions, and statements
- ❑   Iteration and decision-making
- ❑   Functions and modules
- ❑   Classes and object-oriented programming

Of course, there is much more to the Python language than what this short chapter has outlined. Much of it you'll discover as you work through the projects in this book.

Let's get started!

Part I
The Projects

2

Directory/File Snapshot Program

Have you ever installed a program and wanted to know exactly what was installed? Programs typically include numerous files and directories — in some cases hundreds. It can be difficult to determine what was put on the system. This can especially be important if, for instance, you are verifying an install to ensure that all the directories and files were placed on the system. Conversely, with an uninstall, you want to verify just the opposite — that everything that had been put on the system is now gone.

The File/DirectoryComparison program enables you to create a "snapshot" of your system based on a directory "base" you provide. It will also perform a comparison of two snapshots to show you the differences. This includes items missing from snapshot 1 but in snapshot 2, and items missing in snapshot 2 but present in snapshot 1.

Along the way, you'll learn several valuable things about Python and its features:

- ❏ How to create and import modules
- ❏ How to create and call functions
- ❏ Getting user input and passing the value provided by the user to the program
- ❏ How to find information related to the Python Standard Library

Using the Program

You can find the program located on the www.wrox.com page for this book. To run it, simply go to a command prompt, and from the directory on your system where the Chapter 2 program files are located, type the following: **python snapshot.py**.

This will bring up a menu like the one shown here:

```
DIRECTORY/FILE COMPARISON TOOL
======================================
Please type a number and press enter:

1.  Create a snapshot
2.  List snapshot files
3.  Compare snapshots
4.  Help
5.  Exit
```

From here, you can create a snapshot, compare two snapshots, view some help text (always a good idea!), or exit the program. The following sections describe each of the program features.

Creating a Snapshot

There are two scenarios for which you would create a snapshot:

❑   You haven't created a snapshot yet and want to create one to have a "base" to compare against later.

❑   You have created a snapshot and have run some process (such as an install or uninstall) and want to compare it to the first snapshot you created.

In both cases, the interface is the same. When you type **1** and press Enter to create a snapshot, you are prompted for some information the program needs to create it. First, you'll get the following prompt:

```
Enter the directory name to create a snapshot of:
```

This prompt is asking you for the "root" on which to base your snapshot. For instance, if I were installing a program into the normal Windows location (which is C:\Program Files), which creates a directory called jimsprogram, for this prompt I would initially type C:\Program Files because I want to know anything that was put *into* that directory. That way, when my program installs, I can see what has been put into there.

After I tell the directory to "snap," I get the following prompt:

```
Enter the name of the snapshot file to create:
```

In other words, it is creating a file on disk, with the snapshot. This is not a human-readable file (it's a "Pickle" file — more on that later), but Python will be able to read it and use it to compare snapshots. You can give it any valid filename for your system.

Snapshot Filenames

Because you can look up snapshot filenames by extension, it makes sense to use an extension you can remember, and to be consistent. I suggest naming your snapshots with a .snp extension, as that isn't used for any other type of common file.

Your snapshot is now created. Pressing Enter will take you back to the menu.

Listing Snapshot Files

If you type **2** and press Enter, you'll be presented with an option to list the snapshot files in your current directory. Snapshot files can have any valid filename, so you'll be prompted as follows in order for Python to determine how to list the files:

```
LIST SNAPSHOT FILES
=====================================
Enter the file extension for your snapshot files

        (for example, 'snp' if your files end in '.snp'):
```

After you enter the common extension for your snapshot files, you'll be presented with a list similar to the following (except with your own files listed, of course):

```
    Snapshot list:
    =========================

        ci_directory.snp
        ci_directory2.snp
        doctemp1.snp
        doctemp2.snp
Press [Enter] to continue...
```

As noted in the preceding sidebar, don't forget to name all your snapshot files with a consistent extension.

Pressing Enter will take you back to the menu.

Comparing Snapshots

The real purpose of the program is to compare two snapshots to determine what's changed. You'll do this by typing **3** at the menu and pressing Enter. When you do so, you'll get the following prompt:

```
Enter the filename of snapshot 1:
```

Enter the name of the "base" snapshot file (the program looks in the current directory) and press Enter. After you do that, you'll get the following prompt:

```
Enter the filename of snapshot 2:
```

Type the name of the second snapshot file and press Enter. You'll then be presented with results similar to the following:

```
Added Directories:

        new


Added Files:

        jimsworddoc.doc


Removed Directories:

        buildCert


Removed Files:

        !whatsnew.txt
        readme.html
        blueButton.gif
        framed.html
        index.html
        modalPopupTest.html

Press [Enter] to continue...
```

A few notes about the output:

❑ There are four sections to the output:

    ❑ Added directories

    ❑ Added files

    ❑ Removed directories

    ❑ Removed files

❑ If any of the sections have more than 20 items, then the results are shown in tabular format, in three columns.

Pressing Enter will take you back to the menu.

Viewing Help

If you type **4** and press Enter, you'll get the following help screen:

```
DIRECTORY/FILE COMPARISON TOOL
======================================
Welcome to the directory/file snapshot tool.  This tool
allows you to create snapshots of a directory/file tree,
list the snapshots you have created in the current directory,
and compare two snapshots, listing any directories and files
added or deleted between the first snapshot and the second.

To run the program follow the following procedure:
1.  Create a snapshot of a file system to monitor.
2.  Install (or uninstall) a program under test.
3.  Create another snapshot.
4.  Compare the snapshots and note the results.
```

This screen provides a general overview of the program, along with instructions for how to use it. Pressing Enter will take you back to the menu.

Exiting the Program

Well, this one is probably the simplest to understand. Typing **5** and pressing Enter will exit the program and return you to a system prompt.

Putting It All Together

So far, you've seen all the options, but how do you *really* use the program? It involves four basic steps:

1. Create an initial snapshot.

    Let's say you have a program called "Jim's Cool App" (not the most inventive title, but it's 6:00 A.M. after an all-nighter). Suppose also that the program creates a directory in C:\Program Files called JimsCoolApp. The first thing you would do is create a snapshot of C:\Program Files (this is before you install your program).

    Call the snapshot file something meaningful, and probably date it. This example uses 110607-ProgFiles-Base.snp (the current date as I write this).

2. Install your program.

    This one's pretty self-explanatory. Make sure you install to the default location, in the most standard way possible.

3. Create a second snapshot.

    At this point you have created a "base" snapshot and installed your program. It's time to create a snapshot post-install. Run the program again, type **1**, and press Enter to create a snapshot, again naming it something meaningful, in this case 110607-ProgFiles-JCAInstalled.snp.

    At this point, if you want to make sure you named your snapshot files correctly, you can choose option 2 from the menu and list snapshot files.

4. Compare snapshots.

    Finally, you're ready to compare snapshots. Type **3** and press Enter from the menu. First enter the name of the initial snapshot file, 110607-ProgFiles-Base.snp in this case. Then, enter the name of the second snapshot file, which was 110607-ProgFiles-JCAInstalled.snp in the example above.

You'll now be presented with a list of all the files and directories added with "Jim's Cool App."

Other Applications of the Program

Two other possible uses for this program, other than documenting an install, are as follow:

❑   Document an uninstall. In this case, you would just use the "installed" snapshot as your base, and then take another snapshot after uninstalling and compare them to see what was removed. Typically, you would compare the "before install" snapshot to the "after uninstall" snapshot to determine whether the uninstall neglected to delete program artifacts.

❑   If you have a "standard configuration" for a system, you could create a base snapshot with your standard configuration and run the compare after building other systems, to ensure that the list of files and directories is consistent.

Design

The design of the Directory/File Snapshot program is a simple one: It includes two modules, snapshot and snapshothelper, and no classes. Snapshot is the main program, and snapshothelper contains helper functions to perform various tasks, as shown in Figure 2-1.

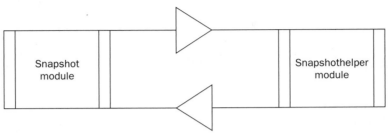

Figure 2-1

No Classes?

This program could have been developed with classes, but recall that in this book I want to show you how to create both procedural and object-oriented code. Therefore, the classes come later.

How It All Fits Together

As mentioned earlier, the snapshot module is the main program, and the one that users will actually run from the command line. It displays the menu, accepts input from the user based on the menu options, and performs actions based on that selection. Generally, the main "actions" that happen as a result of the user's menu selection happen in the snapshothelper module.

The first place that Python looks for a module when it is imported is in the same directory as the main calling program. If a module has been created that is a "helper" module, then that's the logical place to put it. That's why snapshot and snapshothelper are in the same directory.

> If a module is not specific to a particular program, but contains functions and classes you would want to use in many different programs, the best place to put it would be in your Python library directory.

You'll find that this design is quite common — a single "main" program supported by one (or several) "helper" programs that contain classes, functions, or data that provides some kind of service to the calling program. The advantage of this is that it provides *abstraction*. In other words, you can simply call a function from the main program and as long as it provides what you are asking for, it doesn't matter how it was accomplished. This makes modifying programs much easier. You'll learn more about that later.

Main Program

Although the main program for this application is in the `snapshot` module, which displays the menu, accepts the user input, and then calls the appropriate function based on the choice the user made, the functions to actually "do stuff" are not in the `snapshot` module, but rather in `snapshothelper`.

Main Programs in Python

Because Python is an interpreted language with procedural (read: Perl and C) ancestors, the "main" part of a Python program is simply that part of the program you directory run from the command line that is not tied to another structure (such as a class or a function). In other words, if the first program line of your Python module says

```
print "this is the first line"
```

then that is the first line that would be executed, and is effectively the start of your program.

Modules

For this application, there are two modules, the `snapshot` module (the main program) and the `snapshothelper` module.

snapshot Module

In addition to being the main program that users will run, the `snapshot` module also contains the code for displaying the menu and responding to user selections. Table 2-1 shows the function used in the snapshot module.

Table 2-1

Function	Return Type	Description
menu()	string	Displays a menu and receives a user selection through keyboard input; returns the selection to the calling program

snapshothelper Module

The `snapshothelper` module contains the functions that do most of the "heavy lifting" for the program. They essentially provide services, in the form of functions, to the main program when called upon. Table 2-2 describes the functions in the `snapshothelper` module.

Table 2-2

Function	Return Type	Description
createSnapshot()	none	Takes a directory path and chosen snapshot filename and creates a snapshot of the indicated directory, naming the file the chosen filename
listSnapshots()	none	Takes a chosen snapshot file extension and displays to the user a list of snapshot files in the current directory
compareSnapshots()	none	Takes the names of two snapshot files and compares them, outputting to the user a list of all added and removed directories and files between the first snapshot and the second
showHelp()	none	Displays to the user a help screen that displays general program information, as well as suggested steps for using the program
invalidChoice()	none	Returns an error if the user enters an invalid choice
printList()	none	This is a helper function that formats and prints a list of items found. It is used by `compareSnapshots()` and `listSnapshots()`.

Code and Code Explanation

In this section, you'll dive into the details of the code itself. First you'll learn how the `snapshot` and `snapshothelper` modules work together, and some principles of design that will help you to architect well-organized, maintainable Python solutions. You'll also look at some specific functions from the Python Standard Library that I've used in this program, and learn how you can use them in your own applications.

Snapshot.py

The `snapshot` module, as the main program, is the one users will actually run from the command line. As described previously, it contains the code to display the main menu and make decisions based on which menu option the user chooses.

Here's the code for the entire module. Take a general look at it, and then we'll break down the code section by section.

> The following code uses `cls` to clear the screen because this code was written for a Windows system. If you are running on another operating system, you will need to use whatever command is appropriate to clear the screen.

```
#=======================================#
#SNAPSHOT.PY                            #
#DIRECTORY/FILE SYSTEM SNAPSHOT PROGRAM #
#BY JAMES O. KNOWLTON, COPYRIGHT 2007   #
#=======================================#

import sys, os, snapshothelper


#MENU
def menu():
    os.system('cls')
    print '''
DIRECTORY/FILE COMPARISON TOOL
===================================
Please type a number and press enter:

1.  Create a snapshot
2.  List snapshot files
3.  Compare snapshots
4.  Help
5.  Exit
'''
    choice = raw_input("\t")
    return choice

#MENU DECISION STRUCTURE
choice = ""
while choice != "5":
    choice = menu()
    if choice == "1":
        os.system('cls')
        print '''CREATE SNAPSHOT
===================================='''
        directory = raw_input \
                ("Enter the directory name to create a snapshot of: ")
        filename = raw_input \
                ("Enter the name of the snapshot file to create: ")
        snapshothelper.createSnapshot(directory, filename)
    elif choice == "2":
        os.system('cls')
        print '''
```

28

```
        LIST SNAPSHOT FILES
        =====================================
        Enter the file extension for your snapshot files
        (for example, 'snp' if your files end in '.snp'):
        '''
        extension = raw_input("\t\t")
        snapshothelper.listSnapshots(extension)
elif choice == "3":
        os.system('cls')
        print '''
        COMPARE SNAPSHOTS
        =====================================
        '''
        snap1 = raw_input("Enter the filename of snapshot 1: ")
        snap2 = raw_input("Enter the filename of snapshot 2: ")
        snapshothelper.compareSnapshots(snap1, snap2)
elif choice == "4":
        snapshothelper.showHelp()
else:
        if choice != "5":
                snapshothelper.invalidChoice()
```

That's the big picture. The following sections break this down section by section.

Program Header

This first part is quite simply a program header:

```
#========================================#
#SNAPSHOT.PY                             #
#DIRECTORY/FILE SYSTEM SNAPSHOT PROGRAM  #
#BY JAMES O. KNOWLTON, COPYRIGHT 2007    #
#========================================#
```

When writing any code, including Python, it's always a good idea to create a *header,* which is just a formatted comment at the top of the source code file, indicating who wrote it, and what it's for. It's likely you are already familiar with this standard practice, but it is included here once to be thorough. From now on, we'll skip over the header in each source file.

Import Statements

In Python, quite often the first line of executable code you'll see in a source file is an import statement:

```
import sys, os, snapshothelper
```

In this case, you are importing three modules: the standard modules os and sys, and our helper module snapshothelper. Notice that the module we created is imported in the same way as the modules from the Standard Library (those that are included with Python). In fact, if you navigate to the lib directory under your Python program, you'll actually find `os.py` and `sys.py`, which are the python files (modules) you're importing. You can even open them in IDLE and look at them if you're curious.

Make sure that you don't edit these files unless you know what you're doing — otherwise, you could mess something up and the module could become unusable.

The Main Program

We're going to skip over the `menu()` function for now because it actually makes more sense to do so, to follow the flow of the program.

> ### Why Functions Are at the Top
> ### (and the Main Program Is at the Bottom)
>
> Python is an interpreted language. That means instead of "compiling" program files into a single binary file (or a set of binary files), it interprets the source code line by line and executes it (there's actually more to it than that, but you'll find out more about that later). If the main program is at the top of a file and calls a function which is at the bottom, Python hasn't read the function in yet, and therefore doesn't know about it. In order to be able to call a function, it has to be read by Python first.

The first thing the main program does is create a string variable called `choice` and assign it to nothing:

```
choice = ""
```

Although Python is a dynamically typed language (meaning it interprets the data types of members based on their context), variables still have to be assigned some kind of value before they can be used. That's why you have this line — to create memory space for a string variable called `choice`. If for some reason you want to initialize a variable but don't want to give it an initial value, you can assign it to `None`, as in the following example:

```
X = None
```

Next, you create a `while` loop that will form the bulk of your decision tree:

```
while choice != "5":
    choice = menu()
    if choice == "1":
        os.system('cls')
        print '''CREATE SNAPSHOT
======================================'''
        directory = raw_input \
                ("Enter the directory name to create a snapshot of: ")
        filename = raw_input \
```

```
                        ("Enter the name of the snapshot file to create: ")
            snapshothelper.createSnapshot(directory, filename)
    elif choice == "2":
        os.system('cls')
        print '''
        LIST SNAPSHOT FILES
        =====================================
        Enter the file extension for your snapshot files
        (for example, 'snp' if your files end in '.snp'):
        '''
        extension = raw_input("\t\t")
        snapshothelper.listSnapshots(extension)
    elif choice == "3":
        os.system('cls')
        print '''
        COMPARE SNAPSHOTS
        =====================================
        '''
        snap1 = raw_input("Enter the filename of snapshot 1: ")
        snap2 = raw_input("Enter the filename of snapshot 2: ")
        snapshothelper.compareSnapshots(snap1, snap2)
    elif choice == "4":
        snapshothelper.showHelp()
     else:
        if choice != "5":
            snapshothelper.invalidChoice()
```

The `while` loop checks for the `choice` variable being assigned to the string `"5"`.

```
while choice != "5":
```

Because the first time through the `choice` variable is an empty string, the `while` loop will execute at least once. The first thing it does is assign the variable `choice` to the return value of the function `menu()`:

```
choice = menu()
```

> *For information on what the* `menu()` *function does and how it does it, see the section on the* `menu()` *function.*

Once the variable `choice` has been assigned a value (based on actions taken while the `menu()` function was run), the program determines what to do based on the user's menu selection. Because there is no `case` or `switch` statement in Python, the same functionality is developed through a series of `if-elif` statements. At the end, there is an `else` statement, which is the "fallback" option.

If the user enters **1**, the program prompts the user to input a snapshot directory and filename for the snapshot file, respectively, and then assigns those values to variables (through the `raw_input()` function). It then executes the `createSnapshot` function, which is in the `snapshothelper` module:

```
if choice == "1":
        os.system('cls')
        print '''CREATE SNAPSHOT
        ==================================='''
        directory = raw_input \
                ("Enter the directory name to create a snapshot of: ")
        filename = raw_input \
                ("Enter the name of the snapshot file to create: ")
        snapshothelper.createSnapshot(directory, filename)
```

Notice that the module name has to be entered first, followed by the function name, in dot notation. If a function resides in the same module where it is being called (such as the `menu()` function in this module), then the module name is not required. The values of the two entered variables are passed to the function as parameters.

If the user enters **2**, the program prompts the user for the extension they have used for their snapshot files. This response is assigned to a variable (again through the `raw_input` command) and the `listSnapshots` method in `snapshothelper` is called, passing the snapshot file extension to it:

```
elif choice == "2":
        os.system('cls')
        print '''
        LIST SNAPSHOT FILES
        ===================================
        Enter the file extension for your snapshot files
        (for example, 'snp' if your files end in '.snp'):
        '''
        extension = raw_input("\t\t")
        snapshothelper.listSnapshots(extension)
```

If the user enters **3**, the user is prompted for the names of the two snapshot files to compare. Then the `compareSnapshots` function is called, passing the names of the snapshot files as parameters:

```
elif choice == "3":
        os.system('cls')
        print '''
        COMPARE SNAPSHOTS
        ===================================
        '''
        snap1 = raw_input("Enter the filename of snapshot 1: ")
        snap2 = raw_input("Enter the filename of snapshot 2: ")
        snapshothelper.compareSnapshots(snap1, snap2)
```

If the user enters **4**, the `showHelp` method in `snapshothelper` is called, which simply displays the help text.

```
elif choice == "4":
    snapshothelper.showHelp()
else:
    snapshothelper.invalidChoice()
```

What if the user enters **5**? Well, remember our `while` loop? It only executes *while* `choice` does not equal 5. If the user enters **5**, then it breaks out of the loop, and because there is no more code outside the `while` loop, the programs ends.

The menu() Function

Let's now look at the `menu()` function, as control is passing to it at this point:

```
#MENU
def menu():
    os.system('cls')
    print '''
    DIRECTORY/FILE COMPARISON TOOL
    ====================================
    Please type a number and press enter:

    1.  Create a snapshot
    2.  List snapshot files
    3.  Compare snapshots
    4.  Help
    5.  Exit
    '''
    choice = raw_input("\t")
    return choice
```

As you can see, the first thing the menu program does is clear the screen by accessing the `os.system()` function. Remember when we imported the `os` module? This is why. Importing a module enables you to use its resources. The `os` module is especially useful, as it gives you access to operating system resources. For example, the `os.system()` function enables you to run any command you could run at a system prompt (such as `cls` to clear the screen on a Windows command prompt).

After clearing the screen, print a menu to it. Notice the three single-quote characters used in this `print` statement (`'''`). This convention enables you to create a multi-line message and have Python output it exactly as you type it.

As you can see from the menu that's displayed, the user is presented with five options:

- ❑ Create a snapshot file.
- ❑ List the snapshot files in the current directory.
- ❑ Compare snapshots.
- ❑ Display a help screen.
- ❑ Exit.

Then the local variable `choice` is assigned to the output of the `raw_input()` function. The `raw_input()` function is a built-in function that has tremendous value. It enables you to prompt the user and then assign what they type (after they press Enter) to a variable. In this case, we're already presenting the menu, so we don't want to put anything in the message of the `raw_input()` command, but we do want to move the cursor over a bit, so we can insert an escape character for a tab (`"\t"`) in the parameter for the prompt. This moves the cursor to where we want it.

The final line of the `menu()` function returns a value to the code that called it — in this case, returning the string representing the user's selection.

```
return choice
```

snapshothelper.py

The `snapshothelper` module does not have directly executable code of its own — if you ran Python's `snapshothelper.py` at the command prompt, nothing would happen. What it contains is the functions that are used by the snapshot program to do its work.

The module starts with an `import` statement to import all the modules it will be using, and then starts into the functions. Let's go through them one at a time.

createSnapshot(directory, filename)

The `createSnapshot()` function takes a directory (to create the snapshot for) and a filename (the name of the snapshot file), and creates a snapshot file. Take a look at it in its entirety, and then we'll go through it piece by piece:

```
def createSnapshot(directory, filename):
    cumulative_directories = []
    cumulative_files = []

    for root, dirs, files in os.walk(directory):
        cumulative_directories = cumulative_directories + dirs
        cumulative_files = cumulative_files + files

    try:
        output = open(filename, 'wb')
        pickle.dump(cumulative_directories, output, -1)
        pickle.dump(cumulative_files, output, -1)
        output.close()
    except:
        print "Problems encounted trying to save snapshot file!"

    raw_input("Press [Enter] to continue...")
    return
```

The first thing it does is initialize two lists, one to hold a cumulative list of directories and another to hold a cumulative list of files:

```
cumulative_directories = []
cumulative_files = []
```

You then iterate through the chosen directory and build a list of all the directories and files found, using the useful os.walk() function:

```
for root, dirs, files in os.walk(directory):
        cumulative_directories = cumulative_directories + dirs
        cumulative_files = cumulative_files + files
```

At this point you have two lists — cumulative_directories[] has all the directories found, and cumulative_files[] has all the files found. However, you need some way to persistently store these data structures, in order to be able to refer to them later. The pickle module is the perfect solution. Consider pickles in a jar. They are stored and preserved for later access and use. The same applies here. Because sometimes there are issues saving a file to disk, I decided to put the routine to pickle our lists inside a try/except block, as shown here:

```
try:
        output = open(filename, 'wb')
        pickle.dump(cumulative_directories, output, -1)
        pickle.dump(cumulative_files, output, -1)
        output.close()
    except:
        print "Problems encounted trying to save snapshot file!"
```

This way, if there is a problem, the program won't crash. Instead, you'll get a nice error message. As you can see, the `pickle` routine uses the filename that was entered in the main program in the `snapshot` module to save the file.

The last bit of code simply prompts the user to press Enter and then returns control to the main program:

```
raw_input("Press [Enter] to continue...")
return
```

listSnapshot(extension)

The `listSnapshot()` function lists all the snapshot files in the current directory. It takes in a file extension as a parameter and performs its file search based on that. Here is the code:

```
def listSnapshots(extension):
    snaplist = []
    filelist = os.listdir(os.curdir)
    for item in filelist:
        if item.find(extension) != -1:
            snaplist.append(item)

    print '''
Snapshot list:
========================
'''
    printlist(snaplist)

    raw_input("Press [Enter] to continue...")
```

Where's the Return Statement?

You'll notice with this function that there is no return statement. That's because you only use a return when you have some value to return to the code that called the function. Sometimes (as in this case) a function is asked to do something but isn't asked to return a value.

The first thing it does is initialize a couple of values:

```
snaplist = []
filelist = os.listdir(os.curdir)
```

`snaplist` is an (initially) empty list that will hold the list of snapshot files. In the second line of the preceding code, you run the `os.listdir` to generate a list of files (based on the current directory, thanks to the `os.curdir` member). You assign the output to a list with the identifier `filelist`.

You then run a `for` loop that narrows down the list:

```
for item in filelist:
        if item.find(extension) != -1:
            snaplist.append(item)
```

This `for` loop iterates through each item in the `filelist`. It uses the `find` string method to determine whether the snapshot extension is present. If it is, then the file is added to the list `snaplist`. After the `for` loop is done iterating, `snaplist` contains a list of all the snapshot files.

The next piece of code prints out the snapshot list (for more information on the `printList()` function, see the corresponding section below):

```
print '''
Snapshot list:
========================
'''
printList(snaplist)
```

Control now passes back to the main program.

compareSnapshots(snapfile1, snapfile2)

The `compareSnapshots()` method is the largest in the program, and probably the most important. It takes the names of the snapshot files to compare from the main program as parameters, compares two snapshots, and then displays the differences between the two:

```
def compareSnapshots(snapfile1, snapfile2):

    try:
        pkl_file = open(snapfile1, 'rb')
        dirs1 = pickle.load(pkl_file)
        files1 = pickle.load(pkl_file)
        pkl_file.close()

        pk2_file = open(snapfile2, 'rb')
        dirs2 = pickle.load(pk2_file)
        files2 = pickle.load(pk2_file)
        pk2_file.close()
```

(continued)

37

(continued)

```
    except:
        print "Problems encountered accessing snapshot files!"
        raw_input("\n\nPress [Enter] to continue...")
        return

    result_dirs = list(difflib.unified_diff(dirs1, dirs2))
    result_files = list(difflib.unified_diff(files1, files2))

    added_dirs = []
    removed_dirs = []
    added_files = []
    removed_files = []

    for result in result_files:
        if result.find("\n") == -1:
            if result.startswith("+"):
                resultadd = result.strip('+')
                added_files.append(resultadd)
            elif result.startswith("-"):
                resultsubtract = result.strip('-')
                removed_files.append(resultsubtract)

    for result in result_dirs:
        if result.find("\n") == -1:
            if result.startswith("+"):
                resultadd = result.strip('+')
                added_dirs.append(resultadd)
            elif result.startswith("-"):
                resultsubtract = result.strip('-')
                removed_dirs.append(resultsubtract)

print "\n\nAdded Directories:\n"
printList(added_dirs)
print "\n\nAdded Files:\n"
printList(added_files)
print "\n\nRemoved Directories:\n"
printList(removed_dirs)
print "\n\nRemoved Files:\n"
printList(removed_files)
raw_input("\n\nPress [Enter] to continue...")
```

Let's look at this section by section. The first thing the snapshot does is open the two snapshot files:

```
try:
    pkl_file = open(snapfile1, 'rb')
    dirs1 = pickle.load(pkl_file)
    files1 = pickle.load(pkl_file)
    pkl_file.close()
```

```
        pk2_file = open(snapfile2, 'rb')
        dirs2 = pickle.load(pk2_file)
        files2 = pickle.load(pk2_file)
        pk2_file.close()
    except:
        print "Problems encountered accessing snapshot files!"
        raw_input("\n\nPress [Enter] to continue...")
        return
```

Again, when dealing with files, it makes sense to encapsulate your code inside a `try` block. After opening a pickled file, you assign variable names to the data elements stored in the file. That's exactly what we did here. You encapsulated the retrieval of both files inside a single `try` block for code conciseness. You could have put each one in its own `try` block if you wanted to provide a more specific error message.

The next thing you do is the actual comparison. You have imported Python's `difflib` module in order to be able to compare two strings and show differences, so that's what you implement in these next two lines:

```
result_dirs = list(difflib.unified_diff(dirs1, dirs2))
result_files = list(difflib.unified_diff(files1, files2))
```

As you can see, you `diff` the directories and files, respectively, and assign the differences to the lists: `result_dirs` and `result_files`.

The next task is to separate the added files and directories from the removed files and directories. The `unified_diff()` method we accessed in the code appends a plus sign (+) to any files that have been added, and a minus sign (−) to any files that are missing. Based on that flag, you can parse them out:

```
for result in result_files:
    if result.find("\n") == -1:
        if result[0] == "+":
            resultadd = result.strip('+')
            added_files.append(resultadd)
        elif result[0] == "-":
            resultsubtract = result.strip('-')
            removed_files.append(resultsubtract)

for result in result_dirs:
    if result.find("\n") == -1:
        if result[0] == "+":
            resultadd = result.strip('+')
            added_dirs.append(resultadd)
        elif result[0] == "-":
            resultsubtract = result.strip('-')
            removed_dirs.append(resultsubtract)
```

You basically built two lists based on whether the character found indicates the file (or directory) was added or removed. All that remains is to output the results to the screen:

```
print "\n\nAdded Directories:\n"
printList(added_dirs)
print "\n\nAdded Files:\n"
printList(added_files)
print "\n\nRemoved Directories:\n"
printList(removed_dirs)
print "\n\nRemoved Files:\n"
printList(removed_files)
```

Control then passes back to the main program.

showHelp()

showHelp() is a very simple function. It simply displays the help screen and returns control back to the main program:

```
def showHelp():
    os.system('cls')
    print '''
DIRECTORY/FILE SNAPSHOT TOOL
====================================
Welcome to the directory/file snapshot tool.  This tool
allows you to create snapshots of a directory/file tree,
list the snapshots you have created in the current directory,
and compare two snapshots, listing any directories and files
added or deleted between the first snapshot and the second.

To run the program follow the following procedure:
1.   Create a snapshot
2.   List snapshot files
3.   Compare snapshots
4.   Help (this screen)
5.   Exit

'''
```

As before, it uses the three single-quotes (' ' ') to make it easy to format the display of large blocks of text.

invalidChoice()

This is simply an error-response function that executes when a user has entered the wrong input at the menu. Error-checking is critically important, so we implemented it here:

```
def invalidChoice():
    sys.stderr.write("INVALID CHOICE, TRY AGAIN!")
    raw_input("\n\nPress [Enter] to continue...")
    return
```

The Return Statement

If the return statement doesn't actually return a value, then adding it is entirely voluntary — it doesn't change execution. I just added it here to show that you can, if it makes the code more readable for you.

---

printList()

The printList() method is just a helper method I created to print lists of items found. I created it because in testing the application, I found that without it the file list was displayed in one column, which is fine if you only have five files in the list, but not so fine if you have five hundred:

```
def printList(list):
    fulllist = ""
    indexnum = 1

    if len(list) > 20:
        for item in list:
            print "\t\t" + item,
            if (indexnum)%3 == 0:
                print "\n"
            indexnum = indexnum + 1
    else:
        for item in list:
            print "\t" + item
```

It takes a list as a parameter. If the list contains more than 20 items, then the list is formatted in three columns. If the list contains 20 items or fewer, then the items appear in a single column.

Testing

This program contains three components that could cause potential problems. The following list describes them, including some ideas for how to test them:

❑ **The user interface** — To test this, you could just go through all the menus, entering both valid and invalid information. You could easily automate this process with PyUnit (covered later in the book).

❑ **File I/O** — Save files with valid and invalid names, long filenames, and spaces in filenames. Change file permissions on saved files and see what happens.

❑ **The actual difference calculation** — Use a variety of directories. Try a directory with a lot of files, with long filenames, and so on.

Modifying the Program

There are several ways this project could be enhanced, including the following:

❑ The user interface, while functional, is somewhat crude. This project could even be created as a GUI application (using `Tkinter` or another graphics toolkit).

❑ Instead of allowing the snapshot files to be created with any extension, you could enforce a particular extension. That would simplify things (although it would make the program a little less flexible).

❑ You could allow users to "set" a snapshot directory, enabling them to store their snapshot files somewhere other than the location from which the program is run.

❑ You could store properties such as file size, last modified time, or other details in your snapshot file, to make it even more precise.

Summary

In this chapter, you learned how to build a very useful tool for comparing two different versions of a directory tree and displaying what has changed. This could be useful in many different contexts, such as software testing and configuration management. You also learned some valuable Python skills:

❑ How to create and import modules

❑ How to create and access functions

❑ How to prompt for user input and make decisions in the program based on what the user chooses

❑ What the Python Standard Library is, and how to get documentation on the modules contained in it

3

DVD Inventory System

There is a well-known saying that there are two types of programs: those that are toys and those that access databases. Well, the project in this chapter is not a toy, so that should narrow it down for you. This project will enable you to manage your DVD inventory. It takes advantage of MySQL, a powerful open-source relational database management system (RDMS). Along the way, you'll learn how to do the following:

❑   Work with a database

❑   Connect to a database

❑   Query the database

❑   Add records

❑   Modify records

❑   Delete records

❑   Output information in the database to a CSV file

Why All This Is Important

Basically, when you get right down to it, all a computer does is organize and manipulate chunks of data. Displaying a bitmap? Moving data around. Printing a spreadsheet? Sending bits of data from one location to another. Computers are most meaningful when they are able to sort and arrange that data in a way that aids the imperfect carbon-based life forms who operate them — namely, you and me.

This is where database management systems come in. They take the sets of data that you and I deal with all around us (sports statistics, medicine prescriptions, class rosters, military formations, whatever) and they arrange it in a way that makes sense to us.

In other words, understanding how to use databases is one of the most fundamental things you can learn as a developer.

Using the Program

The program is available for download at www.wrox.com. To run it, simply go to a command prompt, and from the directory on your system where the Chapter 2 program files are located, type **python dvd.py.**

This will bring up a menu like the one shown here:

```
================================
DVD DATABASE
================================
1 - Add a DVD to the database
2 - Search inventory
3 - Modify DVD record
4 - Delete DVD record
5 - Export listing to CSV
6 - Exit
================================

Enter a choice and press enter:
```

From here, as you can see, you can add a DVD to the database, search the inventory for DVDs based on search criteria, modify fields in a DVD record, delete a DVD record, export the list of DVDs to a CSV file, or exit the program. The following sections walk through each of these program features.

Installing MySQL

To install and run the application in this chapter, you'll need to install MySQL and the Python MySQLdb package. You can find instructions for downloading and installing MySQL and MySQLdb in Appendix B. After you do that, run the SQL script included in the program directory to create the table needed for this example.

Once it is installed, create a database and name it DVDCOLLECTION. Then run the following SQL command to create the table we'll use in this exercise:

```
CREATE TABLE 'DVD' (
  'DVD_TITLE' varchar(50) default NULL,
  'DVD_STAR_NAME' varchar(50) default NULL,
  'DVD_COSTAR_NAME' varchar(50) default NULL,
  'DVD_YEAR' varchar(50) default NULL
  'DVD_GENRE' varchar(50) default NULL
);
```

Adding a DVD to the Database

If you choose **1** and press Enter to add a DVD to the database, you'll be asked for the following information:

- ❑   DVD title

- ❑   DVD star name

- ❑   DVD costar name

- ❑   DVD year released

- ❑   DVD genre (drama, horror, comedy, or romance)

The screen will look like the following:

```
================================
ADD A DVD TO THE DATABASE:
================================
Enter the DVD title:  American Gangster
Enter the name of the movie's star:  Denzel Washington
Enter the name of the movie's costar:  Russell Crowe
Enter the year the movie was released:  2007
Enter the genre:
 - 1 for Drama, 2 for horror, 3 for comedy, 4 for romance:
```

In the preceding example, I entered DVD information for *American Gangster* (not on DVD yet, but I'm building my Christmas list). After I type a number corresponding to the genre for the movie (in this case, 1 for drama) and press Enter, I get the following prompt:

```
Record added - press enter to continue:
```

After you press Enter you are returned to the main menu.

When Problems Occur

If you encounter a problem while adding the record (for instance, if you don't provide all the information), you'll get an error message. For example, if you merely press Enter when prompted for the genre, you'll get the following message:

```
================================
ADD A DVD TO THE DATABASE:
================================
Enter the DVD title:  Princess Bride
Enter the name of the movie's star:  Cary Elwes
Enter the name of the movie's costar:  Robin Wright
Enter the year the movie was released:  1987
Enter the genre:
 - 1 for Drama, 2 for horror, 3 for comedy, 4 for romance:
ERROR ADDING RECORD!
Press Enter to return to the menu:
```

Searching the DVD Inventory

If you type **2** and press Enter to search the DVD inventory, you'll be presented with the following prompt:

```
===============================
DVD LOOKUP:
===============================
Enter the criteria to look up by:
1 - Movie title
2 - Star
3 - Costar
4 - Year released
5 - Genre

Type a number and press enter:
```

As you can see, you can look up records based on any of the fields that make up a record. Each lookup is covered in the following sections.

Lookup by Movie Title

If you type **1** and press Enter to search by movie title, you'll get the following prompt:

```
Enter the DVD title to search for:
```

Type the name of the movie exactly as it appears in the database and press Enter. You'll then get the result set output to the screen:

```
===============================
DVD SEARCH RESULTS:
===============================
Title:  American Gangster
Star:   Denzel Washington
Costar: Russell Crowe
Year released:  1995
Genre:  : Drama
===============================


Press enter to continue:
```

Press Enter to be returned to the menu.

Lookup by Star

If you type **2** and press Enter to search by the star's name, you'll get the following prompt:

```
Enter the DVD star name to search for:
```

Type the star's name exactly as it appears in the database and press Enter. You'll then get the result set output to the screen (the following example output shows how it looks if multiple DVDs are returned as a result of the search):

```
===============================
DVD SEARCH RESULTS:
===============================
Title:  Tommy Boy
Star:   Chris Farley
Costar: David Spade
Year:   1995
Genre:  Comedy
===============================
Title:  Black Sheep
Star:   Chris Farley
Costar: David Spade
Year:   1996
Genre:  Comedy
===============================


Press enter to continue:
```

Press Enter to be returned to the menu.

Lookup by Costar

If you type **3** and press Enter to search by the costar's name, you'll get the following prompt:

```
Enter the DVD costar name to search for:
```

Type the costar's name exactly as it appears in the database and press Enter. You'll then get the result set output to the screen, as shown in the following example:

```
===============================
DVD SEARCH RESULTS:
===============================
Title:  Runaway Bride
Star:   Julia Roberts
Costar: Richard Gere
```

(continued)

(continued)

```
Year:    1999
Genre:   Comedy
==============================
Title:  Pretty Woman
Star:   Julia Roberts
Costar: Richard Gere
Year:    1990
Genre:   Comedy
==============================


Press enter to continue:
```

Press Enter to be returned to the menu.

Lookup by Year Released

If you type **4** and press Enter to search by the year in which the movie was released, you'll get the following prompt:

```
Enter the DVD release year to search for:
```

Type the appropriate year and press Enter. You'll then get the result set output to the screen. In the following example, note that both movies shown are released in 1990, the year I entered as search criteria:

```
==============================
DVD SEARCH RESULTS:
==============================
Title:  Pretty Woman
Star:   Julia Roberts
Costar: Richard Gere
Year:    1990
Genre:   Comedy
==============================
Title:  Ghost
Star:   Patrick Swayze
Costar: Demi Moore
Year:    1990
Genre:   Drama
==============================


Press enter to continue:
```

Press Enter to be returned to the menu.

Lookup by genre

If you type **4** and press Enter to search by genre, you'll be presented with the following screen:

```
Enter the genre to search for:
1 - Drama
2 - Horror
3 - Comedy
4 - Romance
```

When you type the number corresponding to the genre you want to search for, you'll get a result set consisting of all DVDs in the database associated with that genre:

```
==============================
DVD SEARCH RESULTS:
==============================
Title:  American Gangster
Star:   Denzel Washington
Costar: Russell Crowe
Year:   2007
Genre:  Drama
==============================
Title:  Ghost
Star:   Patrick Swayze
Costar: Demi Moore
Year:   1990
Genre:  Drama
==============================


Press enter to continue:
```

Press Enter to be returned to the menu.

When Problems Occur

If no records are found, you'll get a screen that indicates that fact:

```
==============================
DVD SEARCH RESULTS:
==============================
NO RECORDS FOUND
==============================


Press enter to continue:
```

If you enter something other than 1–5 when prompted for search criteria, you'll get an appropriate error message:

```
================================
DVD LOOKUP:
================================
Enter the criteria to look up by:
1 - Movie title
2 - Star
3 - Costar
4 - Year released
5 - Genre

Type a number and press enter:  6
ERROR IN CHOICE!
Press Enter to return to the menu:
```

In both error cases, pressing Enter takes you back to the main menu.

Modifying a DVD Record

If you type **3** and press Enter to modify a record, you'll get the following initial prompt:

```
================================
MODIFY A DVD RECORD:
================================

Enter the title of the DVD to modify:
```

Type the name of the movie exactly as it appears in the database. When you do, you'll get the following screen:

```
================================
MODIFY A DVD RECORD:
================================

Enter the title of the DVD to modify:  American Gangster
================================
DVD TO MODIFY:
================================
1 - Title:      American Gangster
2 - Star:       Denzel Washington
3 - Costar:     Russell Crowe
4 - Year:       2007
5 - Genre:      Drama
================================
Type the number for the field
you want to modify and press Enter:
```

As you can see, the program displays the information relating to the movie, whose title you entered, and asks you to indicate which field you'd like to modify. The following sections cover each field.

Modify Title

If you type **1** and press Enter to modify the DVD title, you'll get the following prompt:

```
Enter the new DVD title name:
```

Simply type in the new title that you'd like to use and press Enter. The program will then show you the modified record. In the following example, I had initially misspelled my movie "Amrician Gangster." Therefore, I chose option 3 to modify the name, typed in the name of the movie as it currently appeared in the database, and then changed the title text:

```
===============================
Enter the title of the DVD to modify: Amrician Gangster
===============================
DVD TO MODIFY:
===============================
1 - Title:      Amrician Gangster
2 - Star:       Denzel Washington
3 - Costar:     Russell Crowe
4 - Year:       2007
5 - Genre:      Drama
===============================
Type the number for the field
you want to modify and press Enter:  1
Enter the new DVD title name:  American Gangster
===============================
MODIFIED RECORD:
===============================
1 - Title:      American Gangster
2 - Star:       Denzel Washington
3 - Costar:     Russell Crowe
4 - Year:       2007
5 - Genre       Drama
===============================
Press enter to continue:
```

Press Enter to be returned to the menu.

Modify Star

If you type **2** from the main menu and press Enter to modify the name of the DVD's star, you'll get the following prompt:

```
Enter the new DVD star name:
```

Simply type in what you'd like to modify the star's name to, and then press Enter. The program will then show you the modified record, as in the "modify title" example shown in the preceding section.

Then press Enter and you will be returned to the menu.

Modify Costar

If you type **3** and press Enter to modify the DVD costar name, you'll get the following prompt:

```
Enter the new DVD costar name:
```

Simply type in what you'd like to modify the costar's name to, and then press Enter. The program will then show you the modified record.

Press Enter to return to the menu.

Modify Year

If you type **4** and press Enter to modify the DVD release year, you'll get the following prompt:

```
Enter the new DVD year of release:
```

Simply type in what you'd like to modify the DVD release year to, and then press Enter. The program will then show you the modified record.

Press Enter to return to the menu.

Modify Genre

If you type **5** and press Enter to modify the DVD genre, you'll get the following prompt:

```
Enter the genre to apply to this DVD:
1 - Drama
2 - Horror
3 - Comedy
4 - Romance
Type the number for the genre
you want to apply and press Enter:
```

Type the number corresponding to the genre you'd like to apply to your DVD, and then press Enter. The program will then show you the modified record, as shown in previous examples.

Pressing Enter will return you to the menu.

When Problems Occur

If you enter search criteria that does not match a title in the database, then you'll get an appropriate error:

```
================================
MODIFY A DVD RECORD:
================================

Enter the title of the DVD to modify:   American
THERE WAS A PROBLEM ACCESSING THE RECORD IN THE DATABASE!
Press Enter to continue:
```

Similarly, if you enter invalid data when modifying a record, you'll get an error message, as shown in the following example, where I pressed Enter without entering a value for the genre to apply to a record:

```
================================
Enter the genre to apply to this DVD:
1 - Drama
2 - Horror
3 - Comedy
4 - Romance
Type the number for the genre
you want to apply and press Enter:
THERE WAS A PROBLEM MODIFYING THE RECORD
Press Enter to continue:
```

In both error cases, pressing Enter takes you back to the main menu.

Deleting a DVD Record

If you type **4** and press Enter to delete a DVD record, you'll be presented with the following prompt:

```
================================
DELETE A DVD RECORD:
================================

Enter the title of the DVD to delete:
```

Simply enter the title of the DVD you want to delete, exactly as it appears in the database. When you do so, you'll get a screen like the following:

```
================================
DVD TO DELETE:
================================
Title:   American Gangster
Star:    Denzel Washington
```

(continued)

(continued)

```
Costar: Russell Crowe
Year released:  2007
Genre:   : Romance
===============================

         Are you sure you want to delete?  Enter a choice and press enter
        (Y/y = yes, Anything else = No)
```

If you type **Y** or **y** and press Enter, the record will be deleted and you'll get the following confirmation prompt:

```
Item deleted, press enter to continue:
```

If you type anything else and press Enter, then the record will *not* be deleted, and you'll get the following prompt:

```
Item NOT deleted, press enter to continue:
```

In both cases, after you press Enter you'll be returned to the main menu.

When Problems Occur

If the program is unable to find the record you want to delete, then you will get the following error:

```
THERE WAS A PROBLEM ACCESSING THE RECORD IN THE DATABASE!
Press Enter to continue:
```

Pressing Enter will take you back to the menu.

Exporting the List of DVDs to a CSV File

Often, it can be useful to have a list of the items in your database in a comma-separated value (CSV) file. If you type **5** and press Enter to do that, you'll get the following prompt:

```
===============================
EXPORT DATABASE TO CSV:
===============================
Enter base filename (will be given a .csv extension):
```

Type a base filename (the part before the extension) and press Enter. For example, if I decided to name my csv file jimsdvds.csv, I would type jimsdvds and press Enter. I'd then get the following output:

```
==============================
EXPORT DATABASE TO CSV:
==============================
Enter base filename (will be given a .csv extension):  jimsdvds
jimsdvds.csv  successfully written, press Enter to continue:
```

At this point, if I go to the directory from which the program was executed, I will see a `jimsdvds.csv` file. If I bring that file up in a spreadsheet that can read CSV files, I'll see what's shown in Figure 3-1.

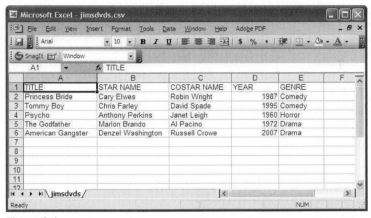

Figure 3-1

Design

Like the example in the previous chapter, the DVD Inventory program uses a text-based menu system (although it is somewhat more complex). The main program is dvd.py, which displays the menu and manages program flow. It calls several other modules:

❑   add_dvds — Adds DVDs to the database

❑   lookup_dvds — Looks up DVDs in the database based on search criteria

❑   modify_dvd — Modifies field information for a particular DVD record

❑   delete_dvd — Deletes DVD records

❑   csvreport_dvd — Generates a CSV file of all the items in the database

---

The Database I Used

For this program, I implemented a MySQL database. However, the application could easily be modified to support any other SQL-compliant database. Simply import the appropriate module for your database and modify the database-connection code. The SQL queries themselves are fairly generic and should work for most databases.

How It All Fits Together

This program differs from the last chapter in one notable way: Instead of a large "helper" module containing all the code branched from the main program, you have created a separate module for each menu option.

One Large Module or Separate Modules?

Basically, this question is a matter of manageability. Because this program is more complex than the File/Directory Snapshot program, with more moving parts, it makes more sense to have a separate module for each menu option. Could you put everything in one module? Yes — and the program would still work. However, I think the current approach makes the program easier to manage and work with.

The short answer? It depends.

Modules

This application has a main module, dvd.py, and multiple modules that are called from the main module. The following sections walk through them one at a time.

dvd.py

In addition to being the main program that users will run, the dvd.py module also contains the code to display the menu and respond to user selections. Table 3-1 shows the function of the dvd.py module.

Table 3-1

Function	Return Type	Description
Menu()	string	Displays a menu and receives a user's selection through keyboard input; returns the choice to the calling program

add_dvd.py

The add_dvd module adds a DVD record to the database. It takes user input for the DVD information and then executes a SQL INSERT statement to insert the record in the database. Table 3-2 describes the functions of the add_dvd module.

Table 3-2

Function	Return Type	Description
AddDVD()	none	Takes user input on title, star, costar, year, and genre and passes that data to SQLAddDVD
SQLAddDVD()	none	Takes title, star, costar, year, and genre information from AddDVD, connects to the database, and inserts the DVD record

lookup_dvds.py

The lookup_dvds module enables the user to look up DVDs in the database by title, star, costar, year, or genre. It also enables finding multiple records if the search returns multiple "hits." Table 3-3 describes the functions of the lookup_dvds module.

Table 3-3

Function	Return Type	Description
LookupDVD()	none	Takes user input on title, star, costar, year, and genre and passes that data to SQLLookupDVD
SQLLookupDVD()	none	Takes title, star, costar, year, and genre information from LookupDVD, connects to the database, and selects the DVD records, displaying them to the user

modify_dvd.py

The modify_dvd module enables the user to modify the fields in a DVD record. It contains just a single function, although the function is quite large. Table 3-4 describes the function of the modify_dvd module.

Table 3-4

Function	Return Type	Description
ModifyDVD()	none	1. Accepts user input for the title of the DVD to modify
		2. Presents the user with the DVD information and prompts for the field to change
		3. Prompts the user for the appropriate value for the selected field
		4. Performs the update against the database and shows the user the updated record

delete_dvd.py

The `delete_dvd` module enables the user to delete a DVD record from the database. Note that deletions are permanent and cannot be undone. Table 3-5 shows the functions of the `delete_dvd` module.

Table 3-5

Function	Return Type	Description
DeleteDVD()	none	Takes user input for the DVD title to delete. Looks up and displays the record. If the user confirms, it calls `SQLDeleteDVD()`, which performs the deletion.
SQLDeleteDVD()	none	This function takes the title from `DeleteDVD()` and performs a SQL `DELETE` on the database for the selected record.

csvreport_dvd.py

The `csvreport_dvd` module takes a filename as user input (the filename to give the report) and writes the database data to a CSV file. Table 3-6 describes the function of the `csvreport_dvd` module.

Table 3-6

Function	Return Type	Description
WriteCSV()	none	Takes a proposed filename from the user and outputs a CSV file of the database contents in the program directory

Code and Code Explanation

As you work through the following code, you'll notice how some items are named similarly — this helps to outline or lay out the structure and makes it easier for those who come after you to read your code. Try to do this whenever you can. Of course, it's not always possible (for example, `modify_dvd.py` has a single function), so make sure you let common sense prevail. Let's look at some code.

In the interests of page space, I've omitted the code headers, but you should make sure that you use them. Your coworkers will thank you.

dvd.py

Basically, the purpose of the main program is to present the user menu and provide branches to the other modules when an item is chosen. The following code example presents the entire program. As you did in the preceding chapter, look it over, and then we'll break it down piece by piece:

```
import os
import add_dvd
import lookup_dvds
import modify_dvd
import delete_dvd
import csvreport_dvd

#MAIN MENU
def Menu():
    os.system('cls')
    print """
    ==============================
    DVD DATABASE
    ==============================
    1 - Add a DVD to the database
    2 - Search inventory
    3 - Modify DVD record
    4 - Delete DVD record
    5 - Export listing to CSV
    6 - Exit
    ==============================
    """
    choice = raw_input("Enter a choice and press enter: ")
    return choice

#TAKE CHOICE AND LAUNCH MODULE
choice = ""
while choice != "6":
    choice = Menu()
    if choice == "1":
        os.system('cls')
        add_dvd.AddDVD()
    elif choice == "2":
        os.system('cls')
        lookup_dvds.LookupDVD()
    elif choice == "3":
        os.system('cls')
        modify_dvd.ModifyDVD()
    elif choice == "4":
        delete_dvd.DeleteDVD()
    elif choice == "5":
        csvreport_dvd.WriteCSV()
```

The main() Function

The main() function (again, main() is implied, even though it's not listed in the program, and anything not in a function or class is part of main() and automatically runs) operates very similarly to the File/Directory Snapshot program: It initializes a choice variable and then uses a while menu, which calls Menu() and assigns the choice variable to menu()'s return value. It then presents the menu and performs actions based on the user's selection:

```
#TAKE CHOICE AND LAUNCH MODULE
choice = ""
while choice != "6":
    choice = Menu()
    if choice == "1":
        os.system('cls')
        add_dvd.AddDVD()
    elif choice == "2":
        os.system('cls')
        lookup_dvds.LookupDVD()
    elif choice == "3":
        os.system('cls')
        modify_dvd.ModifyDVD()
    elif choice == "4":
        delete_dvd.DeleteDVD()
    elif choice == "5":
        csvreport_dvd.WriteCSV()
```

However, note one difference in this case: The while structure has almost no actual code of its own — it simply calls other functions. Here, it calls the functions contained in the other modules pertaining to the menu selections of the user.

Again, the while loop continues to call the menu() function until the user types **6** and presses Enter, which breaks the loop; and because the while loop is the last code in the program, it will end the program and return the user to a system prompt.

Menu()

The Menu() function displays the user menu and accepts the user's input, assigning it to the variable choice:

```
#MAIN MENU
def Menu():
    os.system('cls')
    print """
===============================
DVD DATABASE
===============================
1 - Add a DVD to the database
2 - Search inventory
3 - Modify DVD record
```

```
    4 - Delete DVD record
    5 - Export listing to CSV
    6 - Exit
    ===================================
    """
    choice = raw_input("Enter a choice and press enter: ")
    return choice
```

The function then returns the value of `choice` to the command that called it.

add_dvd.py

The `add_dvd` module adds a DVD record to the database. It has two functions: `AddDVD()`, which interacts with the user, and `SQLAddDVD()`, which interacts with the database. Here's the entire module for you to look at — a breakdown of each function immediately follows:

```
import MySQLdb, random, os

#RUN THE SQL STATEMENT TO INSERT RECORD INTO DATABASE
def SQLAddDVD(Title, Star, Costar, Year, Genre):
    SQL = 'INSERT INTO DVD values ("%s", "%s", "%s", "%s", "%s")' % \

        (Title, Star, Costar, Year, Genre)
    try:
        db = MySQLdb.connect("localhost", "root", "zanzibar", "DVDCOLLECTION")
        c = db.cursor()
        c.execute(SQL)
        db.commit()
        c.close()
        db.close()
        raw_input("Record added - press enter to continue: ")
    except:
        print "THERE WAS A PROBLEM ADDING THE RECORD"
        raw_input("Press Enter to continue: ")

#TAKE USER INPUT AND RUN FUNCTION TO INSERT INTO DATABASE
def AddDVD():
    print "==============================="
    print "ADD A DVD TO THE DATABASE:"
    print "==============================="
    Title = raw_input("Enter the DVD title: ")
    Star = raw_input("Enter the name of the movie's star: ")
    Costar = raw_input("Enter the name of the movie's costar: ")
    Year = raw_input("Enter the year the movie was released: ")
    Genre = raw_input("Enter the genre:\n - 1 for Drama, 2 for horror, \
3 for comedy, 4 for romance: ")
    if Genre == "1":
        Genre = "Drama"
    elif Genre == "2":
        Genre = "Horror"
```

(continued)

(continued)

```
    elif Genre == "3":
        Genre = "Comedy"
    elif Genre == "4":
        Genre = "Romance"
    else:
        print "ERROR GETTING INFORMATION!"
        raw_input("Press Enter to return to the menu: ")
        return


SQLAddDVD(Title, Star, Costar, Year, Genre)
```

AddDVD()

The `AddDVD()` function uses a series of `raw_input` statements to get all the information needed to add a DVD record to the database:

```
Title = raw_input("Enter the DVD title: ")
Star = raw_input("Enter the name of the movie's star: ")
Costar = raw_input("Enter the name of the movie's costar: ")
Year = raw_input("Enter the year the movie was released: ")
```

For genre, because there is a discrete list of items to select from, the user is presented with a list of options and prompted to type a number corresponding to the desired genre. An `if` construct then converts the selected number to the appropriate string value:

```
Genre = raw_input("Enter the genre:\n - 1 for Drama, 2 for horror, \
    3 for comedy, 4 for romance: ")
if Genre == "1":
    Genre = "Drama"
elif Genre == "2":
    Genre = "Horror"
elif Genre == "3":
    Genre = "Comedy"
elif Genre == "4":
    Genre = "Romance"
else:
    print "ERROR GETTING INFORMATION!"
    raw_input("Press Enter to return to the menu: ")
    return
```

As you can see, if the user presses something other than 1–4, then he or she will get an error message.

The last line of the function is simply a call to the `SQLAddDVD()` function, passing it all the values it needs to add the record to the database (Title, Star, Costar, Year, and Genre):

```
SQLAddDVD(Title, Star, Costar, Year, Genre)
```

SQLAddDVD(Title, Star, Costar, Year, Genre)

As you can see from SQLAddDVD()'s parameter list, it takes the data from AddDVD() that the user typed in. Then, the first thing it does is create a string variable to hold the SQL command that will be run to insert the record in the database, using the values provided:

```
SQL = 'INSERT INTO DVD values ("%s", "%s", "%s", "%s", "%s")' % \

        (Title, Star, Costar, Year, Genre)
```

The rest of the function consists of a try/except block for inserting the record in the database:

```
try:
        db = MySQLdb.connect("localhost", "root", "zanzibar", "DVDCOLLECTION")
        c = db.cursor()
        c.execute(SQL)
        db.commit()
        c.close()
        db.close()
        raw_input("Record added - press enter to continue: ")
    except:
        print "THERE WAS A PROBLEM ADDING THE RECORD"
        raw_input("Press Enter to continue: ")
```

It uses the MySQLdb module's connect() method to connect to the MySQL database. Then it assigns to variable c the "cursor" (which is basically the reference point in the database). We then execute the SQL command and commit the changes.

Because connecting to a database and making changes always includes the potential for problems, this code is encapsulated inside a try/except block. When problems occur, an appropriate error message is generated. Pressing Enter will return the user to the main menu.

lookup_dvds.py

The lookup_dvds.py module enables users to query the database with a search pattern and view a list of matching records. It allows searches to be executed based on title, star, costar, year of release, or genre. It is comprised of a LookupDVD() function and a SQLLookupDVD() function. Here is the code:

```
import MySQLdb, os

#RUN THE SQL STATEMENT TO QUERY THE DATABASE
def SQLLookupDVD(searchby, searchtext):
    SQL = "SELECT * FROM DVD WHERE %s = %s" % (searchby, searchtext)
    try:
        db = MySQLdb.connect("localhost", "root", "zanzibar", "DVDCOLLECTION")
        c = db.cursor()
```

(continued)

(continued)

```
            c.execute(SQL)
            output = c.fetchall()
            c.close()
            db.close()
    except:
        print "THERE WAS A PROBLEM ACCESSING THE DATABASE"
        raw_input("Press Enter to continue: ")
        return
    os.system('cls')
    print "==============================="
    print "DVD SEARCH RESULTS:"
    print "==============================="
    if output == ():
        print "NO RECORDS FOUND"
        print "==============================="
    for entry in output:
        print "Title:\t", entry[0]
        print "Star:\t", entry[1]
        print "Costar:\t", entry[2]
        print "Year:\t", entry[3]
        print "Genre:\t", entry[4]
        print "==============================="
    raw_input("\n\nPress enter to continue: ")

#TAKE USER INPUT AND RUN FUNCTION TO QUERY THE DATABASE
def LookupDVD():
    print """
===============================
DVD LOOKUP:
===============================
Enter the criteria to look up by:
1 - Movie title
2 - Star
3 - Costar
4 - Year released
5 - Genre"""

    choice = raw_input("\nType a number and press enter: ")

    searchby = ""
    searchtext = ""
if choice == "1":

        searchby = "DVD_TITLE"

        searchtext = raw_input("Enter the DVD title to search for: ")

        searchtext = "\"%s\"" % (searchtext)
```

```
    elif choice == "2":

        searchby = "DVD_STAR_NAME"

        searchtext = raw_input("Enter the DVD star name to search for: ")

        searchtext = "\"%s\"" % (searchtext)

    elif choice == "3":

        searchby = "DVD_COSTAR_NAME"

        searchtext = raw_input("Enter the DVD costar name to search for: ")

        searchtext = "\"%s\"" % (searchtext)

    elif choice == "4":

        searchby = "DVD_YEAR"

        searchtext = raw_input("Enter the DVD release year to search for: ")

        searchtext = "\"%s\"" % (searchtext)
    elif choice == "5":
        searchby = "DVD_GENRE"
        print """
Enter the genre to search for:
1 - Drama
2 - Horror
3 - Comedy
4 - Romance
"""
        entrychoice = raw_input("\t")
        if entrychoice == "1":
            searchtext = "\"Drama\""
        elif entrychoice == "2":
            searchtext = "\"Horror\""
        elif entrychoice == "3":
            searchtext = "\"Comedy\""
        elif entrychoice == "4":
            searchtext = "\"Romance\""
    else:
        print "ERROR IN CHOICE!"
        raw_input("Press Enter to return to the menu: ")
        return

    SQLLookupDVD(searchby, searchtext)
```

LookupDVD()

The `LookupDVD()` function starts out by simply asking the user which field to search by and assigning it to the variable `choice`:

```
print """
==============================
DVD LOOKUP:
==============================
Enter the criteria to look up by:
1 - Movie title
2 - Star
3 - Costar
4 - Year released
5 - Genre"""

choice = raw_input("\nType a number and press enter: ")
```

Two variables are then initialized as empty strings:

```
searchby = ""
searchtext = ""
```

The next section of the function is an `if` construct that, based on which field the user decided to search on, does two things:

1. It assigns the variable `searchby` to the field the user decided to search on.

2. It prompts the user for the search text and assigns it to the variable `searchtext`:

```
if choice == "1":

        searchby = "DVD_TITLE"

        searchtext = raw_input("Enter the DVD title to search for: ")

        searchtext = "\"%s\"" % (searchtext)
    elif choice == "2":

        searchby = "DVD_STAR_NAME"

        searchtext = raw_input("Enter the DVD star name to search for: ")

        searchtext = "\"%s\"" % (searchtext)
    elif choice == "3":
```

```
            searchby = "DVD_COSTAR_NAME"

            searchtext = raw_input("Enter the DVD costar name to search for: ")

            searchtext = "\"%s\"" % (searchtext)
    elif choice == "4":

            searchby = "DVD_YEAR"

            searchtext = raw_input("Enter the DVD release year to search for: ")

            searchtext = "\"%s\"" % (searchtext)
    elif choice == "5":
        searchby = "DVD_GENRE"
        print """
        Enter the genre to search for:
        1 - Drama
        2 - Horror
        3 - Comedy
        4 - Romance
        """
        entrychoice = raw_input("\t")
        if entrychoice == "1":
            searchtext = "\"Drama\""
        elif entrychoice == "2":
            searchtext = "\"Horror\""
        elif entrychoice == "3":
            searchtext = "\"Comedy\""
        elif entrychoice == "4":
            searchtext = "\"Romance\""
    else:
        print "ERROR IN CHOICE!"
        raw_input("Press Enter to return to the menu: ")
        return
```

As shown in the preceding example, the `if` construct enables users to type in a number corresponding to their selected genre if that is what they are searching on. In addition, there is an `else` branch in case the user provides an invalid entry.

The last thing the function does is call `SQLLookupDVD()`, passing it the field to the search on and the search text:

```
SQLLookupDVD(searchby, searchtext)
```

67

SQLLookupDVD(searchby, searchtext)

The `SQLLookupDVD()` function performs the SQL query to look up any matching records and then outputs the results to the screen. It takes the field to search on and the search text, and creates a string variable with the SQL query:

```
SQL = "SELECT * FROM DVD WHERE %s = %s" % (searchby, searchtext)
```

The next code block is a `try`/`except` block that connects to the database and executes the query, assigning the result set to the variable `output`:

```
try:
    db = MySQLdb.connect("localhost", "root", "zanzibar", "DVDCOLLECTION")
    c = db.cursor()
    c.execute(SQL)
    output = c.fetchall()
    c.close()
    db.close()
except:
    print "THERE WAS A PROBLEM ACCESSING THE DATABASE"
    raw_input("Press Enter to continue: ")
    return
```

With the results assigned to the variable `output`, the function then displays the results to the screen:

```
os.system('cls')
    print "================================"
    print "DVD SEARCH RESULTS:"
    print "================================"
    if not output:
        print "NO RECORDS FOUND"
        print "================================"
    for entry in output:
        print "Title:\t", entry[0]
        print "Star:\t", entry[1]
        print "Costar:\t", entry[2]
        print "Year:\t", entry[3]
        print "Genre:\t", entry[4]
        print "================================"
    raw_input("\n\nPress enter to continue: ")
```

Notice that if the result set is empty, then it prints out a message indicating there are "no records found."

modify_dvd.py

The `modify_dvd` module is the most complex in the program, which is not unexpected — it is much trickier to edit database records in place than to delete them or add them. Here's the whole module. As before, look it over and then we'll break the method down:

```
import MySQLdb

def ModifyDVD():

    print "================================"
    print "MODIFY A DVD RECORD:"
    print "================================"

    dvdTitle = raw_input("\nEnter the title of the DVD to modify: ")

    SQL_LOOKUP = "SELECT * FROM DVD WHERE DVD_TITLE = \"%s\"" % dvdTitle

    try:
        db = MySQLdb.connect("localhost", "root", "zanzibar", "DVDCOLLECTION")
        c = db.cursor()
        c.execute(SQL_LOOKUP)
        searchResult = c.fetchall()
        if searchResult[0] == ():
            raise
    except:
        print "THERE WAS A PROBLEM ACCESSING THE RECORD IN THE DATABASE!"
        raw_input("Press Enter to continue: ")
        return

    try:
        print "================================"
        print "DVD TO MODIFY:"
        print "================================"
        print "1 - Title:\t", searchResult[0][0]
        print "2 - Star:\t", searchResult[0][1]
        print "3 - Costar:\t", searchResult[0][2]
        print "4 - Year:\t", searchResult[0][3]
        print "5 - Genre:\t", searchResult[0][4]
        print "================================"

        choice = raw_input("Type the number for the field \
\nyou want to modify and press Enter: ")

        titleChanged = False
        modify = ""
        newvalue = ""
        if choice == "1":
                modify = "DVD_TITLE"
                newvalueTitle = raw_input("Enter the new DVD title name: ")
                newvalue = "\"%s\"" % newvalueTitle
                titleChanged = True
        elif choice == "2":
            modify = "DVD_STAR_NAME"
            newvalue = raw_input("Enter the new DVD star name: ")
            newvalue = "\"%s\"" % newvalue
        elif choice == "3":
            modify = "DVD_COSTAR_NAME"
            newvalue = raw_input("Enter the new DVD costar name: ")
```

(continued)

(continued)

```
                    newvalue = "\"%s\"" % newvalue
            elif choice == "4":
                modify = "DVD_YEAR"
                newvalue = raw_input("Enter the new DVD year of release: ")
                newvalue = "\"%s\"" % newvalue
            elif choice == "5":
                modify = "DVD_GENRE"
                print "================================="
                print "Enter the genre to apply to this DVD:"
                print "1 - Drama"
                print "2 - Horror"
                print "3 - Comedy"
                print "4 - Romance"

                entrychoice = raw_input("Type the number for the genre \
                \nyou want to apply and press Enter: ")
                if entrychoice == "1":
                    newvalue = "\"Drama\""
                elif entrychoice == "2":
                    newvalue = "\"Horror\""
                elif entrychoice == "3":
                    newvalue = "\"Comedy\""
                elif entrychoice == "4":
                    newvalue = "\"Romance\""

        SQL_UPDATE = "UPDATE DVD SET %s = %s WHERE DVD_TITLE = \"%s\"" \

                    % (modify, newvalue, dvdTitle)

        db = MySQLdb.connect("localhost", "root", "zanzibar", "DVDCOLLECTION")
        c = db.cursor()
        c.execute(SQL_UPDATE)
        db.commit()

        if titleChanged:
                    SQL_LOOKUP = "SELECT * FROM DVD WHERE DVD_TITLE = \"%s\"" %
newvalueTitle

        c = db.cursor()
        c.execute(SQL_LOOKUP)
        modifyResult = c.fetchall()
        c.close()
        db.close()
    except:
        print "THERE WAS A PROBLEM MODIFYING THE RECORD"
        raw_input("Press Enter to continue: ")
        return

    print "================================="
    print "MODIFIED RECORD:"
    print "================================="
    print "1 - Title:\t", modifyResult[0][0]
    print "2 - Star:\t", modifyResult[0][1]
```

70

```
print "3 - Costar:\t", modifyResult[0][2]
print "4 - Year:\t", modifyResult[0][3]
print "5 - Genre\t", modifyResult[0][4]
print "================================="
raw_input("Press enter to continue: ")
```

ModifyDVD()

The function starts out simply enough — it prints the header for the "modify" screen:

```
print "================================="
print "MODIFY A DVD RECORD:"
print "================================="
```

Then the user is prompted for the title of the DVD to be modified, and the response is assigned to the variable dvdTitle:

```
dvdTitle = raw_input("\nEnter the title of the DVD to modify: ")
```

Users need to be able to see what they are modifying, so the first thing you need to do is look up the record:

```
SQL_LOOKUP = "SELECT * FROM DVD WHERE DVD_TITLE = \"%s\"" % dvdTitle

try:
    db = MySQLdb.connect("localhost", "root", "zanzibar", "DVDCOLLECTION")
    c = db.cursor()
    c.execute(SQL_LOOKUP)
    searchResult = c.fetchall()
    if searchResult[0] == ():
        raise
except:
    print "THERE WAS A PROBLEM ACCESSING THE RECORD IN THE DATABASE!"
    raw_input("Press Enter to continue: ")
    return
```

As before, using a try/except block is well-advised when accessing a database, just in case problems occur. As you can see from the preceding code block, if no results are found from the search, then you raise an exception, which displays an error message and returns to the main menu.

Now you are at the bulk of the function — when you actually modify the record. This entire part is encased in a try/except block.

First, display a menu asking users which field they want to modify (and assign their answer to the variable `choice`):

```
print "================================"
print "DVD TO MODIFY:"
print "================================"
print "1 - Title:\t", searchResult[0][0]
print "2 - Star:\t", searchResult[0][1]
print "3 - Costar:\t", searchResult[0][2]
print "4 - Year:\t", searchResult[0][3]
print "5 - Genre:\t", searchResult[0][4]
print "================================"

choice = raw_input("Type the number for the field \
\nyou want to modify and press Enter: ")
```

The next part is a branching section with a nested `if` statement:

```
titleChanged = False
modify = ""
newvalue = ""
if choice == "1":
        modify = "DVD_TITLE"
        newvalueTitle = raw_input("Enter the new DVD title name: ")
        newvalue = "\"%s\"" % newvalueTitle
        titleChanged = True
elif choice == "2":
    modify = "DVD_STAR_NAME"
    newvalue = raw_input("Enter the new DVD star name: ")
    newvalue = "\"%s\"" % newvalue
elif choice == "3":
    modify = "DVD_COSTAR_NAME"
    newvalue = raw_input("Enter the new DVD costar name: ")
    newvalue = "\"%s\"" % newvalue
elif choice == "4":
    modify = "DVD_YEAR"
    newvalue = raw_input("Enter the new DVD year of release: ")
    newvalue = "\"%s\"" % newvalue
elif choice == "5":
    modify = "DVD_GENRE"
    print "================================"
    print "Enter the genre to apply to this DVD:"
    print "1 - Drama"
    print "2 - Horror"
    print "3 - Comedy"
    print "4 - Romance"

    entrychoice = raw_input("Type the number for the genre \
    \nyou want to apply and press Enter: ")
    if entrychoice == "1":
        newvalue = "\"Drama\""
    elif entrychoice == "2":
```

```
            newvalue = "\"Horror\""
    elif entrychoice == "3":
            newvalue = "\"Comedy\""
    elif entrychoice == "4":
            newvalue = "\"Romance\""
```

Did you notice that there are a few variables assigned at the top of this code snippet? The first one is very important. Because all the fields can be changed when a record is modified, you need to ensure that you can redisplay the record after you're done if the field you used to look it up has changed. To do so, you have to monitor whether the title is being modified, and keep track of the title as it appeared originally. That way, you can be sure to display the same record.

The following code does the actual update of the record:

```
SQL_UPDATE = "UPDATE DVD SET %s = %s WHERE DVD_TITLE = \"%s\"" \
        % (modify, newvalue, dvdTitle)

db = MySQLdb.connect("localhost", "root", "zanzibar", "DVDCOLLECTION")
c = db.cursor()
c.execute(SQL_UPDATE)
db.commit()
```

At this point, our `SQL_LOOKUP` string variable contains the value of the DVD title originally entered. If you didn't modify the title, that's fine. However, if you did modify the title, then you need to change the query. Therefore, you next put in a simple little `if` statement:

```
if titleChanged:

        SQL_LOOKUP = "SELECT * FROM DVD WHERE DVD_TITLE = \"%s\"" % newvalueTitle
```

Next, run a query for the modified record and assign its result set to the variable `modifyResult`:

```
c = db.cursor()
c.execute(SQL_LOOKUP)
modifyResult = c.fetchall()
c.close()
db.close()
```

Note that there is an exception statement, like the others you've looked at, displaying an error message if you have a problem with your database connection.

Finally, display the modified record:

```
print "================================"
print "MODIFIED RECORD:"
print "================================"
print "1 - Title:\t", modifyResult[0][0]
print "2 - Star:\t", modifyResult[0][1]
print "3 - Costar:\t", modifyResult[0][2]
print "4 - Year:\t", modifyResult[0][3]
print "5 - Genre\t", modifyResult[0][4]
print "================================"
raw_input("Press enter to continue: ")
```

delete_dvd.py

The `delete_dvd.py` module enables users to delete DVD records from the database. Users will be prompted to ensure that they want to make the deletion, but deletions are permanent. This module includes two functions, `DeleteDVD()` and `SQLDeleteDVD()`, which are described following the code in their entirety:

```
import MySQLdb, os

#RUN THE SQL STATEMENT TO DELETE THE SELECTED RECORD
def SQLDeleteDVD(dvdToDelete):
    try:
                SQL_DELETE = "DELETE DVD FROM DVD WHERE DVD_TITLE = \"%s\"" %
dvdToDelete
        db = MySQLdb.connect("localhost", "root", "zanzibar", "DVDCOLLECTION")
        c = db.cursor()
        c.execute(SQL_DELETE)
        db.commit()
        c.close()
        db.close()
        raw_input("Item deleted, press enter to continue: ")
    except:
        print "THERE WAS A PROBLEM DELETING THE RECORD"
        raw_input("Press Enter to continue: ")


#TAKE USER INPUT AND RUN FUNCTION TO DELETE THE SELECTED RECORD
def DeleteDVD():

    os.system('cls')
    print "================================"
    print "DELETE A DVD RECORD:"
    print "================================"

    dvdToDelete = raw_input("\nEnter the title of the DVD to delete:\t")
            SQL_DELETE = "DELETE DVD FROM DVD WHERE DVD_TITLE = \"%s\"" %
dvdToDelete
```

```
try:
    db = MySQLdb.connect("localhost", "root", "zanzibar", "DVDCOLLECTION")
    c = db.cursor()
    c.execute(SQL_LOOKUP)
    searchResult = c.fetchall()
    if searchResult[0] == ():
        raise
except:
    print "THERE WAS A PROBLEM ACCESSING THE RECORD IN THE DATABASE!"
    raw_input("Press Enter to continue: ")
    return

print "================================"
print "DVD TO DELETE:"
print "================================"
print "Title:\t", searchResult[0][0]
print "Star:\t", searchResult[0][1]
print "Costar:\t", searchResult[0][2]
print "Year released:\t", searchResult[0][3]
print "Genre:\t:", searchResult[0][4]
print "================================"
print '''
Are you sure you want to delete?  Enter a choice and press enter
(Y/y = yes, Anything else = No)
'''
choice = raw_input("\t")

if (choice == "Y" or choice == "y"):
    SQLDeleteDVD(dvdToDelete)
else:
    c.close()
    db.close()
    raw_input("Item NOT deleted, press enter to continue: ")
```

DeleteDVD()

The `DeleteDVD()` function prompts users for the title of the DVD they want to delete, shows them the record, makes sure that they want to delete it, and (assuming they confirm), calls the `SQLDeleteDVD()` function to make the deletion.

It starts by simply displaying the banner for the menu:

```
os.system('cls')
print "================================"
print "DELETE A DVD RECORD:"
print "================================"
```

Then, the user is prompted for the title of the DVD to be deleted, and this information is assigned to the variable `dvdToDelete`:

```
dvdToDelete = raw_input("\nEnter the title of the DVD to delete:\t")
```

A SQL query is then built (so the record can be looked up) and assigned to a variable:

```
SQL_LOOKUP = "SELECT * FROM DVD WHERE DVD_TITLE = \"%s\"" % dvdToDelete
```

The record is then looked up and the result set assigned to a variable:

```
try:
        db = MySQLdb.connect("localhost", "root", "zanzibar", "DVDCOLLECTION")
        c = db.cursor()
        c.execute(SQL_LOOKUP)
        searchResult = c.fetchall()
        if searchResult[0] == ():
            raise
    except:
        print "THERE WAS A PROBLEM ACCESSING THE RECORD IN THE DATABASE!"
        raw_input("Press Enter to continue: ")
        return
```

Again, use `try/except` because you are accessing the database.

Now it's time to display the record to the user and confirm whether they *really* want to delete it:

```
    print "==============================="
    print "DVD TO DELETE:"
    print "==============================="
    print "Title:\t", searchResult[0][0]
    print "Star:\t", searchResult[0][1]
    print "Costar:\t", searchResult[0][2]
    print "Year released:\t", searchResult[0][3]
    print "Genre:\t:", searchResult[0][4]
    print "==============================="
    print '''
Are you sure you want to delete?  Enter a choice and press enter
(Y/y = yes, Anything else = No)
'''
    choice = raw_input("\t")
```

At this point, the function does its work based on what the user input:

```
if (choice == "Y" or choice == "y"):
        SQLDeleteDVD(dvdToDelete)
    else:
        c.close()
        db.close()
        raw_input("Item NOT deleted, press enter to continue: ")
```

If the user selects **Y** or **y** and presses Enter, then the `SQLDeleteDVD()` function is called, passing the title of the DVD to delete. If the user types anything else, then an error message is displayed and the user is returned to the main menu.

SQLDeleteDVD(dvdToDelete)

This function takes the title of the DVD to delete from `DeleteDVD()` and executes the deletion. Because the function is fairly short and straightforward, it is shown in its entirety here:

```
def SQLDeleteDVD(dvdToDelete):
    try:
        SQL_DELETE = "DELETE DVD FROM DVD WHERE DVD_TITLE = \"%s\"" % dvdToDelete
        db = MySQLdb.connect("localhost", "root", "zanzibar", "DVDCOLLECTION")
        c = db.cursor()
        c.execute(SQL_DELETE)
        db.commit()
        c.close()
        db.close()
        raw_input("Item deleted, press enter to continue: ")
    except:
        print "THERE WAS A PROBLEM DELETING THE RECORD"
        raw_input("Press Enter to continue: ")
```

Basically, it takes the title through a parameter, builds a SQL statement, connects to the database, runs the statement, and closes the connection. Because it's in a `try/except` block, if problems are encountered when connecting to the database, then a friendly error message is displayed.

csvreport_dvd.py

The `csvreport_dvd.py` module enables users to export the complete list of DVDs to a CSV file, which can then be retrieved and used in a spreadsheet program. It consists of a single function, `WriteCSV()`. Here is the code:

```
import MySQLdb, csv, os

#FUNCTION TO WRITE ENTIRE DVD LIST TO CSV
def WriteCSV():

    SQL = "SELECT * FROM DVD"

    try:
        db = MySQLdb.connect("localhost", "root", "zanzibar", "DVDCOLLECTION")
        c = db.cursor()
        c.execute(SQL)
        output = c.fetchall()
        c.close()
        db.close()
    except:
        print "THERE WAS A PROBLEM ACCESSING THE DATABASE!"
        raw_input("Press Enter to return to the menu: ")
        return
```

(continued)

(continued)

```
    try:
        os.system('cls')
        print "================================"
        print "EXPORT DATABASE TO CSV:"
        print "================================"
        filename = raw_input("Enter base filename (will be given a .csv extension): ")
        filename = filename + ".csv"
        writer = csv.writer(open(filename, "wb"))
        writer.writerow(("TITLE", "STAR NAME", "COSTAR NAME", "YEAR", "GENRE"))
        writer.writerows(output)
        print filename, " successfully written, press Enter to continue:   "
        raw_input("")
        return
    except:
        print "ERROR WRITING FILE!"
        raw_input("Press Enter to return to the menu: ")
```

WriteCSV()

The program begins by assigning to a string variable a SQL statement to query all records in the database:

```
SQL = "SELECT * FROM DVD"
```

Following this is a `try/except` block to query for all the records in the database, assigning the result set to variable output:

```
    try:
        db = MySQLdb.connect("localhost", "root", "zanzibar", "DVDCOLLECTION")
        c = db.cursor()
        c.execute(SQL)
        output = c.fetchall()
        c.close()
        db.close()
    except:
        print "THERE WAS A PROBLEM ACCESSING THE DATABASE!"
        raw_input("Press Enter to return to the menu: ")
        return
```

Finally, a `try/except` block does the following:

❑ Prompts the user for the filename to use

❑ Uses Python's `csv` module (which we imported) to take the tuple of values (assigned to identifier output) and export them to a `csv` file with the filename the user input

❑ Provides the user with success status when the file has been written

```
try:
        os.system('cls')
        print "================================"
        print "EXPORT DATABASE TO CSV:"
        print "================================"
        filename = raw_input("Enter base filename (will be given a .csv extension): ")
        filename = filename + ".csv"
        writer = csv.writer(open(filename, "wb"))
        writer.writerow(("TITLE", "STAR NAME", "COSTAR NAME", "YEAR", "GENRE"))
        writer.writerows(output)
        print filename, " successfully written, press Enter to continue:   "
        raw_input("")
        return
except:
        print "ERROR WRITING FILE!"
        raw_input("Press Enter to return to the menu: ")
```

Testing

Database programs can be tricky to test. As you test them, you'll want to think about implementing the following tactics:

❏   Test each field individually with several different data sets — use valid data, invalid data, and valid data right at the "boundary" (e.g., if a field can hold integers up to 10,000, then enter 10,000 and 10,001).

❏   Test with "user scenarios," — that is, consider what some typical records or data sets would look like and use those.

❏   Learn how to create export files with your database of choice so you can quickly import them to seed your database. This will save a great deal of time.

Modifying the Program

There are several ways this project could be enhanced, including the following:

❏   You could implement a web interface for the product — in chapter 8, you'll look at Plone, a Python-based web framework designed for just this kind of project.

❏   You could expand on the reporting capabilities — for example, you could enable users to create specific queries for building CSV files.

❏   You could include a field for "rating" and then export it to a CSV file and produce a graph in Excel showing comparisons of different groups of DVDs.

Summary

In this chapter, you learned how to write an application to access and integrate with a database. You learned how to search for information, add records, modify records, and delete records — all from Python. This knowledge serves as a foundation that can help you to build countless applications.

To build truly useful programs with Python, you'll also have to know how to combine the power of a database with the accessibility of computer networks, which is exactly what you'll learn next.

Web Performance Tester

So far, the programs we've written have been useful, but they've shared one main limitation — they are largely self contained, intended to be run on a single computer (although the database program could certainly have a database housed on another computer). Our next program will change that.

The Web Performance Tester has two main functions (I use "function" in the generic sense here):

❑ It will use Python's `urllib2` module to emulate a web browser, access several well-known web sites, and report the amount of time it took to get back the HTML from the page accessed. It will also write its results to a log file, which can be accessed later.

❑ It will communicate with a simple `Python` web server on another machine on the computer's internal network, download a text file and a binary file (through HTTP), and report the results. It will record the results in a `logfile`.

Why Is This Application Important?

Much of the work done by computers is done over networks. Whether it is browsing web pages, connecting to terminal servers via telnet, downloading files via FTP, or performing some other network task, connecting to other computers is one of the most vital tasks a computer performs today.

Using Python, you can act as a server for many of the most popular Internet protocols: HTTP (Web), FTP (File Transfer), Telnet (Remote login), SMTP (Mail service), and SNMP (Network Management), just to name a few.

This application demonstrates how to use Python and its rich collection of modules to interface with a network.

Using the Program

The application is available for download from www.wrox.com. There are actually two separate programs that are run in this application: the Python web server and the Web Performance client.

Running the Python Web Server

Before you run the Python web server, you'll need to determine what port you want to run it on. It needs to be a port that isn't being used by some other program. This chapter's example uses port 8006.

You will want to run the Python web server from any server that you want to monitor for HTTP response performance. To run it, you just need to open a command prompt window and navigate to the Chapter 4 application directory and type **python webserver.py 8006**.

Notice that you need to type the name of the program, followed by the port number as a command-line argument (sometimes called a *parameter*). Later in the chapter you'll learn how to implement command-line arguments in your Python code so that users can "feed" the program customized information when they run your program.

When you run the program, a simple window will be displayed, as shown in Figure 4-1.

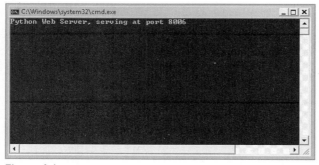

Figure 4-1

To test the web server, bring up your browser and type the following in your browser's address control:

http://localhost:8006/testpage.html.

You should get a page that displays the following text (by the way, this is the quintessential Python philosophy, known as "The Zen of Python," and it can be viewed if you simply type **import this** at a Python interpreter prompt):

```
This is a test page for the Python Web Server.

The Zen of Python, by Tim Peters:

Beautiful is better than ugly.
Explicit is better than implicit.
Simple is better than complex.
Complex is better than complicated.
Flat is better than nested.
Sparse is better than dense.
Readability counts.
Special cases aren't special enough to break the rules.
Although practicality beats purity.
Errors should never pass silently.
Unless explicitly silenced.
In the face of ambiguity, refuse the temptation to guess.
There should be one-- and preferably only one --obvious way to do it.
Although that way may not be obvious at first unless you're Dutch.
Now is better than never.
Although never is often better than right now.
If the implementation is hard to explain, it's a bad idea.
If the implementation is easy to explain, it may be a good idea.
NameSpaces are one honking great idea -- let's do more of those!
```

The web server window should show a line like the following:

```
jim-PC - - [04/Dec/2007 21:42:08] "GET /testpage.html HTTP/1.1" 200 -
```

At this point, the web server is now up and running. Start this for all the servers on your network on which you'd like to test HTTP performance.

When Problems Occur

If for some reason the web server is not able to load, you will get an appropriate error message, which is what happened when I loaded the web server on my machine that was already running a web server on port 8080.

```
There was a problem starting the webserver at port 8080
```

Running the Performance Profiler Client

You can find this application on the Wrox website (www.wrox.com). To run the client, simply type the following: **python webperf.py**.

When you do, you'll be presented with the following menu:

```
=========================================================
WEB PERFORMANCE TESTER
=========================================================
1 - Test client connection to external web sites
2 - Test internal web server performance
3 - Display log file
4 - Exit
=========================================================

        Enter a choice and press enter:
```

You have four options: Connect to external websites and observe the performance from your client machine; connect to internal Python web servers to observe internal HTTP network performance; display the log file in Notepad; and exit. The following sections examine each option.

Testing Connection Performance to External Websites

If you type **1** and press Enter to test connection performance to external websites, you'll be presented with the following prompt:

```
=========================================================
WEB PERFORMANCE TESTER - EXTERNAL SITE CHECK
=========================================================

Enter the websites to check, separated by spaces:
```

For example, to connect to amazon.com, novell.com, and harvard.edu, you would type the following, respectively: **www.amazon.com, www.novell.com, www.harvard.edu**, which results in the following output:

```
=========================================================
WEB PERFORMANCE TESTER - EXTERNAL SITE CHECK
=========================================================

Enter the websites to check, separated by spaces:

www.amazon.com www.novell.com www.harvard.edu

Tue, 04 Dec 2007 22:06:28
Site www.amazon.com took 2.36 seconds to load
Site www.novell.com took 0.26 seconds to load
Site www.harvard.edu took 0.66 seconds to load


Press Enter to Continue:
```

As shown in the preceding output, the results show you exactly how long each site took to load.

Where's the Browser?

You may be wondering how it loaded those websites when you didn't see a browser load! Part of the magic of Python is that it has a module (urllib2) that can retrieve web pages through Hypertext Transfer Protocol (HTTP), just the way a web browser does. By doing it through Python, you are saved the overhead of actually loading the browser, and the benchmark is a truer test of the speed of the actual HTTP response delivered to your client machine.

If there is a problem connecting to a website (such as not being able to find the website), then the user will get an appropriate error, including the name of the problem website:

```
Error connecting to site www.lkdsjflkdsajf.com
```

Testing Internal Web Server Performance

If you type **2** at the main menu and press Enter to test internal web server performance, you'll get the following prompt:

```
==========================================================
WEB PERFORMANCE TESTER - INTERNAL WEBSERVER CHECK
==========================================================


Enter the ip addresses of the web servers
running the Python Webserver, seperated by spaces:
```

For example, if you had two servers running the Python web server and their IP addresses were 192.168.1.102 and 192.168.1.103, at the prompt you would type the following:

```
192.168.1.102 192.168.1.103
```

When I typed the preceding addresses and pressed Enter, the following result displayed in the client program:

```
==========================================================
WEB PERFORMANCE TESTER - INTERNAL WEBSERVER CHECK
==========================================================


Enter the ip addresses of the web servers
running the Python Webserver, seperated by spaces:
```

(continued)

(continued)

```
        192.168.1.102 192.168.1.103
Enter the port the web server is listening on:  8006

Tue, 04 Dec 2007 22:18:20
192.168.1.102:
textfile.txt   took 9.09 seconds to load
binaryfile.exe   took 9.12 seconds to load
192.168.1.103:
textfile.txt   took 0.03 seconds to load
binaryfile.exe   took 0.04 seconds to load


Press Enter to Continue:
```

As you can see, the program downloads both a text file and a binary file from each web server (both text files and binary files are supplied and need to be kept in the same directory as `webserver.py`). The program reports on the amount of time each file took to load, for each web server indicated.

> **For both of these options, note that each test run displays a date-time stamp. This is also output to the log file.**

If a problem occurs when connecting to one of the servers (such as the server crashed and is no longer running), the user will get an appropriate error, with the IP address of the server in question:

```
Error connecting to server 192.168.1.102
```

Displaying the Log File

When profiling and testing web performance, it is critical to be able to view historical data. This enables you to see trends. Moreover, if there are problems, you can go back and see when the problems started. You can also monitor the effects of changes on performance.

If you type **3** and press Enter to view the log file, the program will launch Windows Notepad and bring up the file (if you are running on Linux or Mac, it is easy enough to modify the program to launch `vi` or `TextMate` or whatever editor you prefer).

When connecting to external websites, the log entry written to the log file will have a date-time stamp and the result of all the connection attempts, successful or not, and how long it took to connect, as shown in the following example:

```
Tue, 04 Dec 2007 20:44:38
Site www.novell.com took 0.36 seconds to load
Site www.microsoft.com took 0.15 seconds to load
Error connecting to site www.dlkjdflkjf.com
```

When connecting to internal web servers, the log entry written to the log file will have a date-time stamp and the result of all the connection attempts, successful or not, and how long it took to connect, as shown in the following example:

```
Tue, 04 Dec 2007 22:48:25
192.168.1.103:
textfile.txt took 0.01 seconds to load
binaryfile.exe took 0.02 seconds to load
192.168.1.102:
Error connecting to server 192.168.1.102
```

For example, in my running program, if I choose to view the log file, this is what is displayed in Notepad:

```
Tue, 04 Dec 2007 20:44:38
Site www.novell.com took 0.36 seconds to load
Site www.microsoft.com took 0.15 seconds to load
Error connecting to site www.dlkjdflkjf.com


Tue, 04 Dec 2007 20:44:55
192.168.1.103:
textfile.txt took 0.01 seconds to load
binaryfile.exe took 0.02 seconds to load
1.1.1.1:
Error connecting to server 1.1.1.1


Tue, 04 Dec 2007 20:47:44


Tue, 04 Dec 2007 22:06:28
Site www.amazon.com took 2.36 seconds to load
Site www.novell.com took 0.26 seconds to load
Site www.harvard.edu took 0.66 seconds to load


Tue, 04 Dec 2007 22:18:20
192.168.1.102:
textfile.txt took 9.09 seconds to load
binaryfile.exe took 9.12 seconds to load
192.168.1.103:
```

(continued)

(continued)

```
textfile.txt took 0.03 seconds to load
binaryfile.exe took 0.04 seconds to load


Tue, 04 Dec 2007 22:26:45
Error connecting to site www.lkdsjflkdsajf.com


Tue, 04 Dec 2007 22:29:17
192.168.1.102:
Error connecting to server 192.168.1.102
```

As you can see, each activity is logged to the log file (the file is called `logfile.txt` and is stored in the same directory as the client program).

When Problems Occur

Typically, problems won't occur because all this option does is open the log file. However, if for some reason the log file is not there, then Notepad will simply prompt the user to create it.

Design

There are actually two components to this program: the server component and the client component. In this respect, it is similar to many network applications (such as Telnet, SMTP mail, FTP, HTTP, and so on). The components are laid out thus:

❑   `webserver.py` is the web server, and it runs on a server on which you want to check HTTP response performance. It imports other standard library modules, but no other modules that are part of this application. It does use `textfile.txt`, `binaryfile.exe`, and `testpage.html` to facilitate testing.

❑   `webperf.py` is the main client program that is run. It displays the menu, accepts user selections, and does some work, but mostly it calls functions in `webclient.py`.

❑   `webclient.py` has the modules that comprise the "guts" of the client application. Its modules are called by `webperf.py`.

Test Files

Three support files are included in the chapter's source code folder: `textfile.txt`, `binaryfile.exe`, and `testpage.html`. They need to exist in the directory where you put `webserver.py` on your server. You can replace them with other files if you like (if you want to download a larger file, for example), but your new file will have to be named the same in order for the program to work.

How It All Fits Together

Although this program does not have as much actual code as some of the other examples, it is more complex in one significant way. Whereas all the programs have used multiple modules, this is the first program for which the user actually runs two different programs. Often an "application" will consist of more than one program that a user runs, and this chapter's project is a good example.

Modules

This application has three modules, one for the web server and two for the client. The following sections look at these in turn.

webserver.py

The webserver.py module takes the port number to start the web server as a command-line argument and starts the web server, displaying status activity messages to standard output. Table 4-1 shows the function of the webserver.py module.

> *This function could have just been run as part of the main program, but by encapsulating it in a function it can now be imported and called if necessary from another program.*

Table 4-1

Function	Return Type	Description
RunServer()	none	Executes a Python-based web server

webperf.py

The webperf.py module presents the user menu and launches the appropriate functions from webclient.py based on user menu options. Table 4-2 shows the function of the webperf.py module.

Table 4-2

Function	Return Type	Description
Menu()	string	This takes the user's selection, based on menu options, and returns it to the main program, which launches it.

webclient.py

The webclient.py module connects to either external websites or internal web servers based on which function is called, and presents the results both to the screen and to the log file. Table 4-3 shows the functions of the webclient module.

Table 4-3

Function	Return Type	Description
CheckExternalSites()	none	Takes a list of external sites (passed to it from the main program in webperf.py) and attempts to connect to each site, reporting to the screen and the log file success or failure, and how long the connection took.
CheckInternalWebServers()	none	Takes a list of internal web servers (passed to it from the main program in webperf.py) and attempts to connect to each site, reporting to the screen and the log file success or failure, and how long the connection took.

Code and Code Explanation

As you examine the code, you may begin to form preferences for how to do things, and those preferences may be slightly different from mine. For example, I name functions with the first letter of each word capitalized. That's one way to do it, but you could also use underscores, such as function_name, or just use lowercase — Python doesn't care. However, for readability, you should be consistent in these stylistic decisions. Always think of the code reader, who may be someone other than you.

Let's look at some code.

webserver.py

As mentioned earlier, webserver.py is run on your server. It starts a lightweight Python-based web server at the port you designate. As usual, we'll look at the entire program, and then go through it section by section:

```
import SimpleHTTPServer, SocketServer, sys

#SET THE PORT VARIABLE TO COMMAND-LINE ARGUMENT
PORT = sys.argv[1]

def RunServer():
    try:
        httphandler = SimpleHTTPServer.SimpleHTTPRequestHandler

        httpd = SocketServer.TCPServer(("", int(PORT)), httphandler)

        print "Python Web Server, serving at port" + PORT
        httpd.serve_forever()
```

```
    except (KeyboardInterrupt, SystemExit):
        print "Exiting..."
        sys.exit
    except:
        print "There was a problem starting the webserver at port " + PORT

RunServer()
```

Looks pretty simple, doesn't it? That's the beauty of Python — difficult tasks suddenly become easy.

Main()

The main part of the program does three things. First, it imports the `SimpleHTTPServer` and `SocketServer` modules (along with `sys`), which are the Python modules that provide HTTP server support:

```
import SimpleHTTPServer, SocketServer, sys
```

Second, it assigns the first command-line argument to the variable `PORT`:

```
#SET THE PORT VARIABLE TO COMMAND-LINE ARGUMENT
PORT = sys.argv[1]
```

Third, after the function code (remember, a function has to be read in before it can be called), the main program calls the `RunServer()` function:

```
RunServer()
```

RunServer()

`RunServer()` is the main part of the Python web server. As I said earlier, this could have been part of the main program, but sometimes it is nice to encapsulate code in functions simply so that you can call that function later from another program, should you want to.

Here's the code for the function:

```
def RunServer():
    try:
        httphandler = SimpleHTTPServer.SimpleHTTPRequestHandler

        httpd = SocketServer.TCPServer(("", int(PORT)), httphandler)

        print "Python Web Server, serving at port", PORT
        httpd.serve_forever()
    except:
        print "There was a problem starting the webserver at port " + PORT
```

As you can see, the running of the web server is encapsulated inside a `try/except` block. This is because anytime you start a server process, issues can arise (for example, the port you've selected could already be in use). Therefore, it's a good idea to use the `try/except` block.

The first thing this function does is create an HTTP request handler object and assign it to the identifier `httphandler`:

```
httphandler = SimpleHTTPServer.SimpleHTTPRequestHandler
```

You then create a TCP server, passing it the port number and the `httphandler` object:

```
httpd = SocketServer.TCPServer(("", int(PORT)), httphandler)
```

You then output a message to the screen indicating that you are starting the service, and run the TCP server's `serve_forever()` method, which actually starts the web server:

```
print "Python Web Server, serving at port", PORT
httpd.serve_forever()
```

If there is a problem, then you have an except block that will handle it and present a nice error message to the user:

```
except:
        print "There was a problem starting the webserver at port " + PORT
```

webperf.py

The `webperf.py` module is the module actually run on the client machine. Here is the code for it:

```
import webclient, os

#MAIN MENU
def Menu():
    os.system('cls')
    print """
    =========================================================
    WEB PERFORMANCE TESTER
    =========================================================
    1 - Test client connection to external web sites
    2 - Test internal web server performance
    3 - Display log file
    4 - Exit
    =========================================================
    """
    choice = raw_input("\tEnter a choice and press enter: ")
    return choice
```

```
#TAKE CHOICE AND LAUNCH MODULE
choice = ""
while choice != "4":
    choice = Menu()
    if choice == "1":
        os.system('cls')
        sites = []
        print """
        ========================================================
        WEB PERFORMANCE TESTER - EXTERNAL SITE CHECK
        ========================================================
        """
        siteresponse = raw_input("\tEnter the websites to check,
separated by spaces:\n\n\t")
        sites = siteresponse.split()
        webclient.CheckExternalSites(sites)
    elif choice == "2":
        os.system('cls')
        servers = []
        print """
        ========================================================
        WEB PERFORMANCE TESTER - INTERNAL WEBSERVER CHECK
        ========================================================
        """
        print """
        Enter the ip addresses of the web servers
        running the Python Webserver, seperated by spaces:\n\t"""
        serverresponse = raw_input("\t")
        servers = serverresponse.split()
        port = raw_input("Enter the port the web server is listening on: ")
        webclient.CheckInternalWebServers(servers, port)
    elif choice == "3":
        os.system("notepad logfile.txt")
```

Notice that `raw_input()` is used differently in the preceding two instances. In the first, `raw_input` includes the prompt to the user. In the second, the user is prompted with a print `statement`, and then the `raw_input` gets the user input. Either can be used — in this case, for the second item I chose to include a print statement first because it was easier to print a multi-line string that way.

Main()

In the code below, on line 3 the `Menu()` function is called, and its return value is assigned to the variable choice. It then uses a `while` loop to present the menu:

```
choice = ""
while choice != "4":
    choice = Menu()
    if choice == "1":
        os.system('cls')
        sites = []
        print """
        ========================================================
        WEB PERFORMANCE TESTER - EXTERNAL SITE CHECK
        ========================================================
        """
        siteresponse = raw_input("\tEnter the websites to check,
separated by spaces:\n\n\t")
        sites = siteresponse.split()
        webclient.CheckExternalSites(sites)
    elif choice == "2":
        os.system('cls')
        servers = []
        print """
        ========================================================
        WEB PERFORMANCE TESTER - INTERNAL WEBSERVER CHECK
        ========================================================
        """
        print """
Enter the ip addresses of the web servers
running the Python Webserver, seperated by spaces:\n\t"""
        serverresponse = raw_input("\t")
        servers = serverresponse.split()
        port = raw_input("Enter the port the web server is listening on: ")
        webclient.CheckInternalWebServers(servers, port)
    elif choice == "3":
        os.system("notepad logfile.txt")
```

Again, the `while` loop continues to call the `Menu()` function until the user types **4** and presses Enter, which will break the loop; and because the `while` loop is the last code in the program, this ends the program and returns the user to a system prompt.

The first two options should be fairly straightforward to you by now. Option 3 simply loads `notepad.exe` and opens the log file. If you want to run a different editor, simply change the parameter for the `os.system()` command.

Menu()

The `Menu()` function displays the user menu and gets the user's input, assigning it to the variable choice:

```
def Menu():
    os.system('cls')
    print """
    ========================================================
    WEB PERFORMANCE TESTER
    ========================================================
    1 - Test client connection to external web sites
    2 - Test internal web server performance
    3 - Display log file
    4 - Exit
    ========================================================
    """
    choice = raw_input("\tEnter a choice and press enter: ")
    return choice
```

The function then returns the value of `choice` to the command that called it.

webclient.py

`webclient.py` contains the functions that do the main processing for the client application. Here is the code for it:

```
from urllib2 import urlopen
import socket, sys, time, datetime

socket.setdefaulttimeout(15)

def CheckExternalSites(sites):
    logfile = open ("logfile.txt", "a")
    logtime = time.strftime("\n%a, %d %b %Y %H:%M:%S")
    print logtime
    logfile.write(logtime + "\n")

    for site in sites:
        try:
            start = time.time()
            data = urlopen("http://" + site)
            stuff = data.read()
            end = time.time()
            difference = end - start
            output = "Site %s took %2.2f seconds to load" %( site, difference )
            logfile.write(output + "\n")
            print output
        except:
            errno, errstr = sys.exc_info()[:2]
            if errno == socket.timeout:
                timeouterror = "there was a timeout"
                logfile.write(timeouterror + "\n\n")
                print timeouterror + "\n"
                raw_input("Press Enter to Continue: ")
```

(continued)

(continued)

```python
                        return
                else:
                        genericerror = "Error connecting to site %s" % (site)
                        logfile.write(genericerror + "\n\n")
                        print genericerror + "\n"
                        raw_input("Press Enter to Continue: ")
                        return
        print "\n"
        logfile.write("\n")
        logfile.close()
        raw_input("Press Enter to Continue: ")

def CheckInternalWebServers(serverlist, port):
        logfile = open ("logfile.txt", "a")
        logtime = time.strftime("\n%a, %d %b %Y %H:%M:%S")
        print logtime
        logfile.write(logtime + "\n")

        textfile = "textfile.txt"
        binaryfile = "binaryfile.exe"
        for server in serverlist:
                try:
                        start = time.time()
                        serveroutput =  server + ":"
                        logfile.write(serveroutput + "\n")
                        print serveroutput
                        for file in textfile, binaryfile:
                                data = urlopen("http://%s:%s/%s") % (server, port, file)
                                stuff = data.read()
                                end = time.time()
                                difference = end - start
                                print file, " took %2.2f seconds to load" %( difference )
                                logfile.write("%s took %2.2f seconds to load" %( file,
difference ) + "\n")
                except:
                        errno, errstr = sys.exc_info()[:2]
                        if errno == socket.timeout:
                                timeouterror = "there was a timeout"
                                logfile.write(timeouterror + "\n\n")
                                print timeouterror
                                logfile.close()
                                raw_input("Press Enter to continue: ")
                                return
                        else:
                                genericerror = "Error connecting to server " + server
                                logfile.write(genericerror + "\n\n")
                                print genericerror
                                raw_input("Press Enter to Continue: ")
                                return
        print "\n"
        logfile.write("\n")
        logfile.close()
        raw_input("Press Enter to Continue: ")
```

> ### Using `from` in Import Statements
>
> On the first line of the preceding code, did you notice I put a twist in the `import` statement for `urllib2`? If you don't want to have to type **'module name'** every time you access a module's properties or methods, you can do this. However, be careful: One problem with using `from` is that you can no longer tell just from looking at a line of code where the property or method is coming from. Another danger when using `from` is that you could run into namespace collisions, whereby you wind up importing a method from an object that has the same name as a method from another object.

The sole line of executable code in this module not tied to a method simply sets the timeout value for the socket connection to 15 seconds:

```
socket.setdefaulttimeout(15)
```

CheckExternalSites(sites)

This function connects to a list of websites passed to it by `webperf.Main()` and reports the results to the screen and to a log file. Here is the code:

```
def CheckExternalSites(sites):
    logfile = open ("logfile.txt", "a")
    logtime = time.strftime("\n%a, %d %b %Y %H:%M:%S")
    print logtime
    logfile.write(logtime + "\n")

    for site in sites:
        try:
            start = time.time()
            data = urlopen("http://" + site)
            stuff = data.read()
            end = time.time()
            difference = end - start
            output = "Site %s took %2.2f seconds to load" %( site, difference )
            logfile.write(output + "\n")
            print output
        except:
            errno, errstr = sys.exc_info()[:2]
            if errno == socket.timeout:
                timeouterror = "there was a timeout"
                logfile.write(timeouterror + "\n\n")
                print timeouterror + "\n"
                raw_input("Press Enter to Continue: ")
                return
            else:
                genericerror = "Error connecting to site %s" % (site)
```

(continued)

(continued)

```
            logfile.write(genericerror + "\n\n")
            print genericerror + "\n"
            raw_input("Press Enter to Continue: ")
            return
    print "\n"
    logfile.write("\n")
    logfile.close()
    raw_input("Press Enter to Continue: ")
```

The first few lines of code open the `logfile` for appending and simply output the formatted date and time to the screen and to the `logfile`:

```
logfile = open ("logfile.txt", "a")
    logtime = time.strftime("\n%a, %d %b %Y %H:%M:%S")
    print logtime
    logfile.write(logtime + "\n")
```

The next block of code is comprised of a `for` loop that iterates through the list of sites passed to the function by the main program. This loop records the time, connects to the site (using `urllib2`'s `urlopen` method), records the time again, and then reports the time difference as an elapsed time:

```
for site in sites:
        try:
            start = time.time()
            data = urlopen("http://" + site)
            stuff = data.read()
            end = time.time()
            difference = end - start
            output = "Site %s took %2.2f seconds to load" %( site, difference )
            logfile.write(output + "\n")
            print output
        except:
            errno, errstr = sys.exc_info()[:2]
            if errno == socket.timeout:
                timeouterror = "there was a timeout"
                logfile.write(timeouterror + "\n\n")
                print timeouterror + "\n"
                raw_input("Press Enter to Continue: ")
                return
            else:
                genericerror = "Error connecting to site %s" % (site)
                logfile.write(genericerror + "\n\n")
                print genericerror + "\n"
                raw_input("Press Enter to Continue: ")
                return
```

As you can see, this is encapsulated in a `try`/`except` block. In this case, the function is checking for a specific exception first (a socket timeout). If that isn't detected, then any other timeouts get a generic error message.

Finally, the function writes its results to the screen and `logfile`:

```
print "\n"
logfile.write("\n")
logfile.close()
raw_input("Press Enter to Continue: ")
```

Note two important things about how the `logfile` is handled:

❑ Every time the function outputs to the screen, it also writes to the `logfile`.

❑ The `logfile` is always closed after it is used.

Why Close the Log File?

Whenever you have a program that logs to a file, it is important to close the log file when you're done with it. The reasons are numerous, but probably the most important is that your computer is using valuable resources to keep files open; in order to be a "good citizen" on your computer with all the other programs, it's an essential practice to return any unused resources to the computer to be used for other things when you're done.

CheckInternalWebServers(serverlist, port)

This function takes the list of servers to check and the port the servers are listening on from `webperf`
`.Main()` and connects to each server. It downloads a canned text file and binary file, and reports how long it took to download each, for each server. If there are errors, then it reports those:

```
def CheckInternalWebServers(serverlist, port):
logfile = open ("logfile.txt", "a")
    logtime = time.strftime("\n%a, %d %b %Y %H:%M:%S")
    print logtime
    logfile.write(logtime + "\n")

    textfile = "textfile.txt"
    binaryfile = "binaryfile.exe"
    for server in serverlist:
        try:
            start = time.time()
            serveroutput =  server + ":"
            logfile.write(serveroutput + "\n")
            print serveroutput
            for file in textfile, binaryfile:
                data = urlopen("http://%s:%s/%s") % (server, port, file)
```

(continued)

(continued)

```
                   stuff = data.read()
                   end = time.time()
                   difference = end - start
                   print file, " took %2.2f seconds to load" %( difference )
                   logfile.write("%s took %2.2f seconds to load" %( file,
difference ) + "\n")
           except:
                   errno, errstr = sys.exc_info()[:2]
                   if errno == socket.timeout:
                       timeouterror = "there was a timeout"
                       logfile.write(timeouterror + "\n\n")
                       print timeouterror
                       logfile.close()
                       raw_input("Press Enter to continue: ")
                       return
                   else:
                       genericerror = "Error connecting to server " + server
                       logfile.write(genericerror + "\n\n")
                       print genericerror
                       raw_input("Press Enter to Continue: ")
                       return
       print "\n"
       logfile.write("\n")
       logfile.close()
       raw_input("Press Enter to Continue: ")
```

As with the other function, the first few lines of code open the `logfile` for appending and simply output the formatted date and time to the screen and to the `logfile`:

```
       logfile = open ("logfile.txt", "a")
       logtime = time.strftime("\n%a, %d %b %Y %H:%M:%S")
       print logtime
       logfile.write(logtime + "\n")
```

It then assigns variables to the text and binary files:

```
       textfile = "textfile.txt"
       binaryfile = "binaryfile.exe"
```

The next block of code is a `for` loop, similar in some ways to the one in the `CheckExternalSites()` function. Again, a `try`/`except` construct is used. For each server, it connects to the web server and attempts to download each type of file via HTTP. If successful, it writes to the screen how long it takes. If an error occurs, then that is handled through an exception (again, either through a socket timeout or a generic exception):

```
       for server in serverlist:
           try:
               start = time.time()
```

```
            serveroutput =  server + ":"
            logfile.write(serveroutput + "\n")
            print serveroutput
            for file in textfile, binaryfile:
                data = urlopen("http://%s:%s/%s") % (server, port, file)
                stuff = data.read()
                end = time.time()
                difference = end - start
                print file, " took %2.2f seconds to load" %( difference )
                logfile.write("%s took %2.2f seconds to load" %( file,
  difference ) + "\n")
        except:
            errno, errstr = sys.exc_info()[:2]
            if errno == socket.timeout:
                timeouterror = "there was a timeout"
                logfile.write(timeouterror + "\n\n")
                print timeouterror
                logfile.close()
                raw_input("Press Enter to continue: ")
                return
            else:
                genericerror = "Error connecting to server " + server
                logfile.write(genericerror + "\n\n")
                print genericerror
                raw_input("Press Enter to Continue: ")
                return
```

Finally, the result is output to the screen and the `logfile` and then the `logfile` is closed:

```
print "\n"
logfile.write("\n")
logfile.close()
raw_input("Press Enter to Continue: ")
```

Other Support Files

It is worth noting a few other files that are part of this application:

❑ `textfile.txt` — This is a text file that is stored in the directory where you run the web server. It is used to test web server performance.

❑ `binaryfile.exe` — This is a text file that is stored in the directory where you run the web server. It is also used to test web server performance.

❑ `testpage.html` — This is an HTML file that is stored in the directory where you run the web server. It is used to verify that the web server is running.

Testing

One difficulty in testing network applications is determining whether the error or problem you are seeing is due to a network problem or a software defect. A good standard practice is to ensure that the program can detect network errors and report them without crashing. With that goal in mind, here are some testing ideas:

❑ When testing external website connections, enter a bogus website name, enter an extremely long website name, or enter an IP address instead of a website name.

❑ When testing internal web server connections, enter a bogus IP address, enter a valid IP address for a server without the web server running, or enter a hostname instead of an IP address.

❑ Delete the `logfile` and try to choose the menu option to bring it up — see what happens. Set the `logfile` to `readonly` and try to write to it — see what happens.

Modifying the Program

There are several ways this project could be enhanced. The following are only a few suggestions:

❑ You could perform multiple types of downloads from the internal web server, such as large files.

❑ You could change the `logfile` to be a `csv` file, so that you could perform analysis in a spreadsheet on performance data.

❑ You could expand the program to also test performance of FTP and Telnet servers.

❑ You could set the program to run entirely through command-line arguments, so that it could be run periodically as a scheduled task.

Summary

This chapter's project explored how to connect to remote computers and perform various operations using Python. The following topics were addressed:

❑ How to build a web server entirely in Python

❑ Connecting to external servers with Python

❑ Managing logging and log files in a Python program

5

Customer Follow-Up System

All the applications examined thus far have involved a character-based user interface, based on characters viewed and typed in a terminal. In this chapter, you will explore using mod_python, an add-on module for the popular open-source Apache web server, to use Python to interact with client users through a web browser.

The Customer Follow-up application will perform two main functions:

❑ It will use the mod_python Apache module to present an HTML form to a client user, and enable users to type in their information (including comments) and submit it.

❑ It will use the Python smtplib module to connect to an SMTP mail server and send an e-mail message to a predefined "webmaster" e-mail address.

❑ For each comment submitted, it will enter a log entry to a csv file stored on the web server machine. This log can then be queried and sorted like any other spreadsheet file.

Using the Program

There are basically two user interfaces to the program: the web page that enables a comment to be entered and e-mailed, and the log file, which can be viewed with any spreadsheet (for the screen shots in this chapter, I used the OpenOffice.org Calc program).

Preliminaries

Before you can use the application, an Apache web server needs to be running, on which `mod_python` is installed and configured. `mod_python` has several different *handlers*, and in the example for this chapter the Publisher handler is used.

What Is a Handler?

In Apache, a *handler* is simply an instruction to the web server to do certain things when it encounters a file of a certain type. For example, there might be a handler that launches Adobe Acrobat Reader when a PDF file is encountered.

There are *implicit* handlers that are built into the web server, and *explicit* handlers that are configurable through the `<web server root>\conf\httpd.conf` file. `mod_python` uses explicit handlers to tell Apache how to handle files with a `.py` extension.

Installing Apache

Apache is the most popular web server on the Internet. It is available for multiple operating systems, including Windows and Linux. Although Apache itself is extremely customizable, the installation of the web server is fairly straightforward.

Although the examples in this chapter are all based on Windows (including the installs), installation on Linux/UNIX is fairly straightforward, and the instructions here can still be used as a basic guide to the order of install steps.

Note also that the Apache Server for Windows is supported on Windows 2000, Windows 2003, and Windows XP (with Service Pack 2 applied), but not on Windows 95, ME, or 98.

To install Apache:

Download Apache (the current version is 2.2) from `http://httpd.apache.org/download.cgi`. When installing on Windows (as in this example), it would be a good idea to review the tips for Windows found at `www.hightechimpact.com/Apache/httpd/binaries/win32/README.html`.

To actually download, go to `www.trieuvan.com/apache/httpd/binaries/`. From there, you will get a directory listing showing folders representing different operating systems, as shown in Figure 5-1.

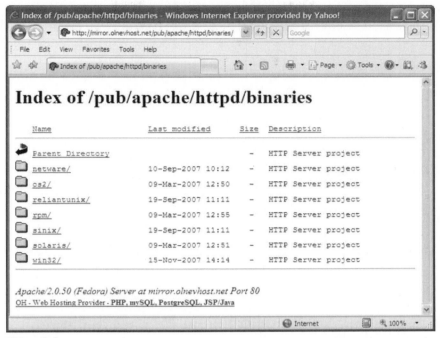

Figure 5-1

Click the Win32 folder. A page will be presented with a list of possible files to download. Assuming version 2.6 is still the latest version, click the file called apache_2.2.6-win32-x86-no_ssl.msi. This will install the Win32 version of Apache 2.2.6, without SSL support (which we don't need for this chapter's project).

> Keep in mind that these instructions are for installing a version of Apache for Windows that will give you the functionality you need to run this chapter's application. Apache is a very robust and configurable web server, and a complete treatment of it is beyond the scope of this book.

Once you've downloaded the file, simply double-click it in Windows Explorer to start the install process. The first screen displays the Welcome page of the Installation Wizard, as shown in Figure 5-2.

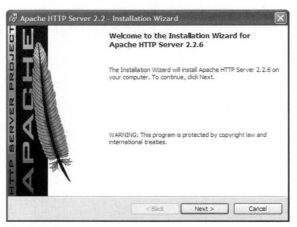

Figure 5-2

Click the Next button to bring up the next screen, the License Agreement page, as shown in Figure 5-3.

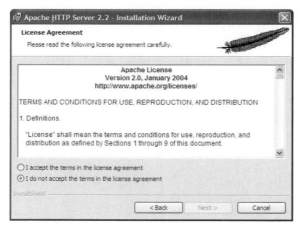

Figure 5-3

Click the "I accept . . . " radio button, and click Next. This will bring up the README information, as shown in Figure 5-4.

Figure 5-4

Click Next to bring up the configuration screen. It will look similar to the dialog shown in Figure 5-5.

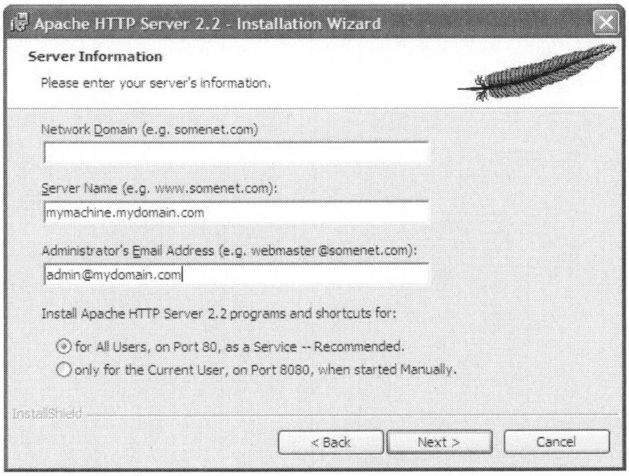

Figure 5-5

Assuming the Apache server is being set up simply to test the application in this chapter, anything can be entered in the Network Domain field (I typed `"www.knowlton.com"`). The other fields should be pre-populated, and they can be left alone. Once the fields have been filled in, click Next, which will bring up the Setup Type screen shown in Figure 5-6.

Figure 5-6

Leave the setup type as Typical and click Next. The Destination Folder window will appear, as shown in Figure 5-7.

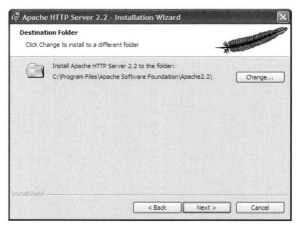

Figure 5-7

Click Next, and then click Install to begin the install. When the install is finished, the dialog shown in Figure 5-8 will appear, indicating that the install is complete.

Figure 5-8

Click Finish to close the install program.

Installing mod_python

Once you have Apache installed, the next step in setting up the system to support Python web applications is to install and configure mod_python.

What Is mod_python?

mod_python is an Apache module that embeds a Python interpreter within the Apache web server. It enables you to integrate the Python language with web content. Using mod_python, you can develop web applications that will often run faster than Common Gateway Interface (CGI) applications and that provide access to advanced features such as maintaining connections to databases and parsing XML. Moreover, all this can be done with the Python language.

To install mod_python:

Download mod_python (the current version as of this writing is 3.3.1) from http://httpd.apache .org/modules/python-download.cgi. Click the link on the page called Win32 Binaries and then download the latest version.

With the file downloaded, simply double-click it to start the installer. Figure 5-9 shows the first screen of the Setup Wizard.

Figure 5-9

Click Next. The next screen, shown in Figure 5-10, enables you to select the directory where Python is located.

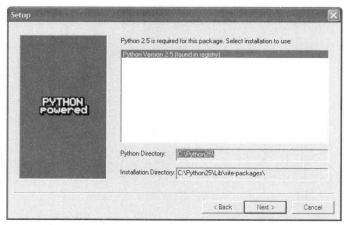

Figure 5-10

Make sure the install is pointing to your Python program directory (it should be), and click Next.

Click Next again to begin the install.

You will be prompted for the location where Apache is installed, as shown in Figure 5-11.

Figure 5-11

Select the Apache program location and click OK. Figure 5-12 shows the final screen of the Setup Wizard.

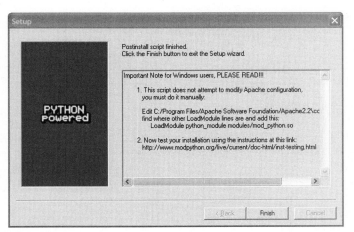

Figure 5-12

Do not close this last window until you have copied the line in item #1 of the confirmation dialog to the clipboard. Once you have done that, click Finish.

Configuring Apache for mod_python

Configuring Apache for `mod_python` involves two steps:

1. Open the `<apache dir>\conf\httpd.conf` file and locate the section where the modules are loaded. You can identify this section easily by the group of lines that all start with `LoadModule`. Paste the line you copied to the clipboard in the preceding section:

```
LoadModule python_module modules/mod_python.so
```

2. In the same file, add the following lines (they can be added anywhere in the file):

```
AddHandler mod_python .py
PythonHandler mod_python.publisher
PythonDebug On
```

Copying Program Files into Their Proper Directories

To set up the application for use, follow these steps:

1. Create a directory called `test` under `<apache dir>\htdocs`.

2. Create a directory named `c:\logs`.

3. Copy `form.py` and `form.html` into the `test` directory.

4. Copy `feedbacklog.csv` into the `c:\logs directory`.

Running the Program

Although there is a significant amount of "under the hood" activity in this application, the interface presented to the user is fairly simple. Basically, users leave comments through their web browser, and the administrator has a CSV log file that can be viewed and sorted.

Entering Comments at the Website

Assuming your Apache web server is running on your local machine, type **http://loalhost/test/form.html** into the address area of your web browser. Figure 5-13 shows the feedback dialog that appears.

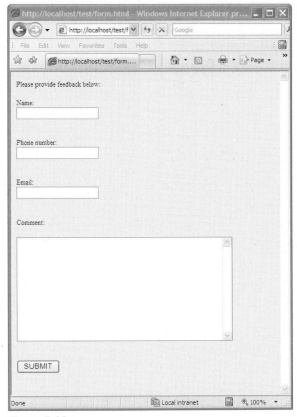

Figure 5-13

Type a name in the Name field (see Figure 5-14).

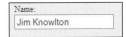

Figure 5-14

Enter a phone number in the Phone number field, as shown in Figure 5-15.

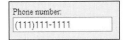

Figure 5-15

Enter an e-mail address in the Email field, as shown in Figure 5-16.

Figure 5-16

Enter some comments in the Comment field, as shown in Figure 5-17.

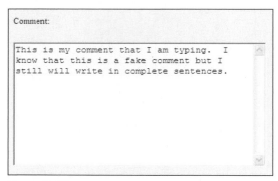

Figure 5-17

Finally, click the Submit button, as shown in Figure 5-18.

Figure 5-18

> **The application assumes you have an SMTP server running on the web server machine. If you don't, you'll get an error right at this point, but don't worry about it — we'll modify the script later to point to your SMTP server.**

The following status message will now display:

```
Dear Jim Knowlton,
Thank You for your kind comments, we will get back to you shortly.
```

When Problems Occur

If the fields are not all filled in, then the following error message will display when Submit is clicked:

```
A required parameter is missing, please go back and correct the error
```

Viewing and Sorting the Log File

On the web server machine, navigate to the c:\logs directory.

In your favorite spreadsheet, retrieve the feedbacklog.csv file. You'll see something similar to the file shown in Figure 5-19 (I have formatted the columns a little for readability).

Figure 5-19

Design

The application has two interfaces: the web page for users to enter and submit comments, and the CSV log file for administrators.

How It All Fits Together

The basic architecture of the program is fairly simple, as shown in Figure 5-20.

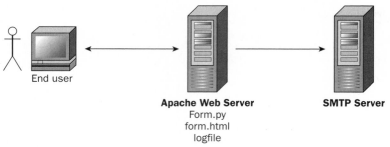

Figure 5-20

The application flows as follows:

❑ The end user connects to the web server to bring up `form.html` (which will be in the `test` subdirectory). This HTML file presents the feedback form.

❑ When the user clicks the Submit button, the HTML file passes the filled-in form information to `form.py`, which it then launches.

❑ `form.py` constructs an e-mail message and sends it to the webmaster, using an SMTP server connection defined in the script.

❑ `form.py` also writes to a CSV log file, which can then be parsed and sorted.

Modules

There is just one module in this program, `form.py`.

form.py

`form.py` is the module that is launched from the `form.html` file. It contains two functions. Table 5-1 shows the functions of the `form.py` module.

Table 5-1

Function	Return Type	Description
`email(req, name, phone, email, comment)`	string	Takes form information from `form.html` and constructs and sends an e-mail message. It returns a successful status message to users through the browser.
`writeCSVLog(name, phone, email, comment)`	none	Takes comment information passed to it and writes log information to a CSV file, along with the current date

Code and Code Explanation

This application might appear to be simple, since there is only one Python source file, but there are several "moving parts," which we'll cover thoroughly.

In the interests of page space, I've omitted the code headers, but make sure you use them. Your coworkers will thank you.

form.html

Although it is not a Python source file, this file is critical to the operation of the program, so it is explored here in its entirety:

```html
<HTML>
<BODY LANG="en-US" BGCOLOR="#ccffff">
<P>Please provide feedback below:
</P>
<FORM ACTION="form.py/email" METHOD="POST">
        <P>Name:<BR> <INPUT TYPE=TEXT NAME="name"><BR><BR><BR>
        </P>
        <P>Phone number:<BR> <INPUT TYPE=TEXT NAME="phone"><BR><BR><BR>
        </P>
        <P>Email:<BR> <INPUT TYPE=TEXT NAME="email"></P>
        <P><BR>Comment:</P>
        <P>
        <TEXTAREA NAME="comment" ROWS=10 COLS=45 STYLE="width: 4in; height:
2in"></TEXTAREA>
        <BR><BR><BR>
        </P>
        <P>INPUT TYPE=SUBMIT VALUE="SUBMIT">
        </P>
</FORM>
</BODY>
</HTML>
```

The <BODY> tag defines the body of the HTML page, and sets the color:

```html
<BODY LANG="en-US" BGCOLOR="#ccffff">
```

Next is some text prompting users so that they know what to do:

```html
<P>Please provide feedback below:
</P>
```

The next line initiates the form, and points to the Python function to run when the form is submitted:

```
<FORM ACTION="form.py/email" METHOD="POST">
```

The next part of the file contains the input fields for the name, phone number, e-mail address, and comment:

```
<P>Name:<BR> <INPUT TYPE=TEXT NAME="name"><BR><BR><BR>
        </P>
        <P>Phone number:<BR> <INPUT TYPE=TEXT NAME="phone"><BR><BR><BR>
        </P>
        <P>Email:<BR> <INPUT TYPE=TEXT NAME="email"></P>
        <P><BR>Comment:</P>
        <P>
        <TEXTAREA NAME="comment" ROWS=10 COLS=45 STYLE="width: 4in;
height: 2in"></TEXTAREA>
        <BR><BR><BR>
        </P>
```

Next is the HTML code for the Submit button:

```
<p><INPUT TYPE=SUBMIT VALUE="SUBMIT">
            </P>
```

The file ends with the closing tags for the different elements in the file:

```
</FORM>
</BODY>
</HTML>
```

form.py

The form.py file is the main "guts" of the program:

```
import smtplib, csv, datetime, sys

WEBMASTER = "jknowlton525@gmail.com"
SMTP_SERVER = "localhost"

def writeCSVLog(name, phone, email, comment):
    python_exec = sys.executable
    if python_exec.find("exe") != -1:
        dir_root = "c:\\logs\\"
    else:
        dir_root = "//usr//local//logs//"
    today = datetime.datetime.now().strftime("%m/%d/%Y")
```

```
            row = [today, name, phone, email, comment]
        try:
            writer = csv.writer(open(dir_root + "feedbacklog.csv", "a"))
            writer.writerow(row)
        except:
            print "There was a problem writing to the logfile!"
            sys.exit
def email(req, name, phone, email, comment):

    # make sure the user provided all the parameters
    if not (name and phone and email and comment):
        return "A required parameter is missing, \
                please go back and correct the error"

    # create the message text
    msg = """\
From: %s
Subject: feedback
To: %s

I have the following comment:

%s

Thank You,

%s
%s

""" % (email, WEBMASTER, comment, name, phone)

    # send it out
    try:
        conn = smtplib.SMTP(SMTP_SERVER)
        conn.sendmail(email, [WEBMASTER], msg)
        conn.quit()
    except:
        print "There was a problem sending the email!"
        sys.exit

    # provide feedback to the user
    s = """\
<html>
<BODY BGCOLOR="#ccffff" DIR="LTR">
Dear %s,<br>
Thank You for your kind comments, we
will get back to you shortly.
</BODY>
</html>""" % name

    writeCSVLog(name, phone, email, comment)
    return s s
```

First, the needed modules are imported:

```
import smtplib, csv, datetime
```

Then variables are declared for the webmaster and the SMTP server:

```
WEBMASTER = "jknowlton525@gmail.com"
SMTP_SERVER = "localhost"
```

> As shown in the preceding code, the program assumes that the SMTP server is running on the same physical machine as the web server. If this is not the case, then you can simply change `localhost` to the hostname or IP address of your SMTP server.

In order to follow the natural flow of the program, let's move down to the `email()` function.

The email(req, name, phone, email, comment)

The e-mail function is the main function for the program. It takes the parameters from the HTML file, sends the e-mail message, and calls the function to write to the log file. Here is the entire function:

```
def email(req, name, phone, email, comment):

    # make sure the user provided all the parameters
    if not (name and phone and email and comment):
        return "A required parameter is missing, \
                please go back and correct the error"

    # create the message text
    msg = """\
From: %s
Subject: feedback
To: %s

I have the following comment:

%s

Thank You,

%s
%s

""" % (email, WEBMASTER, comment, name, phone)
```

```
      # send it out
      try:
          conn = smtplib.SMTP(SMTP_SERVER)
          conn.sendmail(email, [WEBMASTER], msg)
          conn.quit()
      except:
          print "There was a problem sending the email!"
          sys.exit

      # provide feedback to the user
      s = """\
<html>
<BODY BGCOLOR="#ccffff" DIR="LTR">
Dear %s,<br>
Thank You for your kind comments, we
will get back to you shortly.
</BODY>
</html>""" % name

      writeCSVLog(name, phone, email, comment)
      return s
```

This function definition takes its parameters from the HTML file:

```
def email(req, name, phone, email, comment):
```

Following that is an error-checking routine to ensure that all the parameters have been entered:

```
      # make sure the user provided all the parameters
      if not (name and phone and email and comment):
          return "A required parameter is missing, \
                  please go back and correct the error"
```

The next block of code constructs the e-mail message, using information entered into the HTML form by the user:

```
      # create the message text
      msg = """\
From: %s
Subject: feedback
To: %s

I have the following comment:

%s

Thank You,
```

(continued)

(continued)

```
%s
%s

""" % (email, WEBMASTER, comment, name, phone)
```

The next logical step is to send the e-mail message, and that's what is done here:

```
# send it out
try:
    conn = smtplib.SMTP(SMTP_SERVER)
    conn.sendmail(email, [WEBMASTER], msg)
    conn.quit()
except:
    print "There was a problem sending the email!"
    sys.exit
```

The program then writes a message to the user, letting them know the e-mail message was sent:

```
# provide feedback to the user
    s = """\
<html>
<BODY BGCOLOR="#ccffff" DIR="LTR">
Dear %s,<br>
Thank You for your kind comments, we
will get back to you shortly.
</BODY>
</html>""" % name
```

Finally, the `writeCSVLog()` function is called to write the information to the log file:

```
writeCSVLog(name, phone, email, comment)
return s
```

writeCSVLog(name, phone, email, comment)

The `writeCSVLog` function, as the name implies, writes an entry to the log file. Here is the code:

```
def writeCSVLog(name, phone, email, comment):
    python_exec = sys.executable
    if python_exec.find("exe") != -1:
        dir_root = "c:\\logs\\"
    else:
        dir_root = "//usr//local//logs//"
    today = datetime.datetime.now().strftime("%m/%d/%Y")
    row = [today, name, phone, email, comment]
    try:
        writer = csv.writer(open(dir_root + "feedbacklog.csv", "a"))
        writer.writerow(row)
```

The function definition line accepts the required parameters:

```
def writeCSVLog(name, phone, email, comment):
```

It then takes the current date and formats it into a string variable, for use in the log entry:

```
today = datetime.datetime.now().strftime("%m/%d/%Y")
```

The next line is to define a list with the current date and the supplied parameters:

```
row = [today, name, phone, email, comment]
```

Finally, the log file is opened and written to:

```
try:
        writer = csv.writer(open(dir_root + "feedbacklog.csv", "a"))
        writer.writerow(row)
    except:
        print "There was a problem writing to the logfile!"
```

Testing

There are many ways to test web applications. Some ideas are as follows:

❏   Test field data. Remember that each entered field is passed as a parameter to the Python function, so one test would be to enter unexpected data (such as digits for a "name") and see what happens.

❏   Enter large amounts of text and make sure the program doesn't crash.

❏   Test the web page UI itself. For example, minimize and maximize it, resize it, or try it in different browsers.

Modifying the Program

There are several ways this project could be enhanced, including the following:

❏   You could implement an "admin" web UI so that an administrator doesn't have to retrieve the CSV file to view comments entered.

❏   You could store the log information in an XML file or a database so that it is easier to query.

❏   You could create a system to query the log file and send a follow-up e-mail to anyone with comments after a certain number of days.

Summary

In this chapter, you built a web form to take user comments and forward those comments to an e-mail server. You also learned how to set up a simple SMTP (e-mail) server in Python. You explored how to use the csv module to log activity to a comma-separated value (CSV) file. Along the way, you learned the following:

- ❑   How to install Apache's mod_python module
- ❑   How to configure mod_python for your Python interpreter
- ❑   How to create a web form and have it run a Python program in response to user action on the web form
- ❑   How to send an e-mail message entirely through Python

6

Test Management/ Reporting System

In Chapter 3, you learned how to access a database to store and retrieve structured data for use in a Python script, but what about situations where a database is overkill? It is precisely for these kinds of situations that XML exists, and Python is brimming with features to enable you to write to, query, and otherwise manipulate XML.

The test management and reporting system in this chapter shows how you can use XML to store and retrieve structured data in a Python script.

The application will perform the following functions:

- ❑ Enable a user to run tests and report on the pass or fail results of the tests
- ❑ Enable a user to list the test runs, by date
- ❑ Enable a user to show test run results for any previous test run
- ❑ Enable a user to output the results of any completed test run to an HTML file, so that results can be viewed in a web browser

What Are We Testing?

You'll notice as you look at the application that the "program under test" is fairly trivial. That's because the focus of the application is the test framework, not the program that's being tested. It can easily be adapted to a more complex application under test.

Using the Program

You can get to the program by navigating to the directory corresponding to this chapter. As in the previous chapters, the files are available for download from www.wrox.com. To run the application, simply go to a command prompt, and from the directory on your system where the Chapter 6 program files are located, type **python test_manager.py**.

This will bring up a menu like the one shown here:

```
=================================
TEST MANAGEMENT/REPORTING SYSTEM
=================================
1 - Run tests
2 - List test runs
3 - Show test results
4 - Generate HTML test report
5 - Help
6 - Exit
=================================

Enter a choice and press enter:
```

From here, you can run tests, list all completed test runs, show results for any completed test run, generate an HTML test report, view a help screen, or exit the program. The following sections walk through each of the program features.

> You won't be able to do anything with option 2, 3, or 4 until you run tests at least once.

Running Tests

If you choose **1** to run tests, you'll receive the following prompt:

```
=================================
RUN TESTS
=================================

    Enter your first name:
```

The program will prompt for three sets of information. Based on the information supplied by the user, the tests will either pass or fail. Since I wrote the program, I set the "correct" answer for first name to "Jim," so for now, type **Jim** and press Enter.

When you do, you'll get the next prompt:

```
================================
RUN TESTS
================================

    Enter your first name: Jim
    Enter your last name:
```

Type **Knowlton** and press Enter. After you do, you'll get the final prompt:

```
================================
 RUN TESTS
================================

    Enter your first name: Jim
    Enter your last name: Knowlton
    Prime number test - enter a number:
```

The final prompt checks an input number to determine whether it is a prime number. If it is, then the test passes. In order to ensure that all the tests will pass (for now), type the number **2** (a prime number) and press Enter. You'll then see the results of the tests:

```
================================
TEST RUN RESULTS
================================
Test first name - PASSED
Test last name - PASSED
Test prime number - PASSED
================================
Total tests passed:  3
Total tests failed:  0
Total tests with errors:  0

Press [Enter] to continue:
```

As you can see, all the tests passed.

How Test Results Are Stored

The test report is stored in the `test_runs` directory under the program directory, and is saved in the format `mm-dd-yyyy.xml`. In other words, a report of a test run on January 1, 2008 would be stored as `01-01-2008.xml`.

If you open the XML file (which you don't have to do to run the program), it will look like this:

```
<testresult>
    <testfirstname>PASSED</testfirstname>
    <testlastname>PASSED</testlastname>
    <testprimenumber>FAILED - 4 is not a prime number</testprimenumber>
    <testspassed>2</testspassed>
    <testsfailed>1</testsfailed>
    <testserror>0</testserror>
</testresult>
```

What If Some Tests Fail?

If you enter incorrect information in one of the first two prompts and the test fails, the test results indicate a failure and provide troubleshooting information, as shown in the following example:

```
=================================
RUN TESTS
=================================


    Enter your first name: Joe
    Enter your last name: Knowlton
    Prime number test - enter a number: 2


=================================
TEST RUN RESULTS
=================================
Test first name - FAILED - EXPECTED Jim but was Joe
Test last name - PASSED
Test prime number - PASSED
=================================
Total tests passed:  2
Total tests failed:  1
Total tests with errors:  0

Press [Enter] to continue:
```

If you enter a non-prime number for the third test and the test fails, the program shows a failure and simply tells you it is not a prime number:

```
=================================
RUN TESTS
=================================


    Enter your first name: Jim
    Enter your last name: Knowlton
    Prime number test - enter a number: 4


=================================
TEST RUN RESULTS
=================================
```

```
        Test first name - PASSED
        Test last name - PASSED
        Test prime number - FAILED - 4 is not a prime number
        ===================================
        Total tests passed:  2
        Total tests failed:  1
        Total tests with errors:  0

  Press [Enter] to continue:
```

Press Enter to return to the main menu.

Listing Test Runs

To list test runs, type **2** at the menu and you'll get a screen like the following:

```
        ===================================
        LIST TEST RUNS
        ===================================

             01-13-2008
             01-14-2008
             01-15-2008


        ===================================

  Press [Enter] to continue:
```

Press Enter to return to the main menu.

Showing Test Results

If you type **3** and press Enter to show results for a particular test run, you'll get the following prompt:

```
        ===================================
        SHOW TEST RESULTS
        ===================================


  Enter the date of the test run in the
      following format: '01-01-2008'
      (or type 'today' for today)
```

If you enter a date corresponding to an existing test run (you can check what is existing by choosing option 2 to list test runs, as described previously), the results are output in the following screen:

```
=================================
SHOW TEST RESULTS
=================================


Enter the date of the test run in the
    following format: '01-01-2008'
    (or type 'today' for today)


=================================
TEST RUN RESULTS 01-14-2008
=================================
Test first name - PASSED
Test last name - PASSED
Test prime number - FAILED - 4 is not a prime number
=================================
Total tests passed:  2
Total tests failed:  1
Total tests with errors:  0

Press [Enter] to continue:
```

When Problems Occur

If for some reason the program cannot find the test run file, you will get an appropriate error message:

```
=================================
SHOW TEST RESULTS
=================================


Enter the date of the test run in the
following format: '01-01-2008'
01-20-2008


    Problem opening test run file!

Press [Enter] to continue:
```

Press Enter to return to the main menu.

Generating an HTML Test Report

If you type **4** and press Enter to generate an HTML test report, you'll get the following screen:

```
==================================
GENERATE HTML REPORT
==================================


Enter the date of the test run in the
following format: '01-01-2008'
```

Type the date of an existing test run and press Enter. After the report is generated, you will see the following status displayed on the screen:

```
==================================
GENERATE HTML REPORT
==================================


Enter the date of the test run in the
following format: '01-01-2008'
01-14-2008

    -- HTML Report Generated --
    Press [Enter] to continue:
```

The report is stored in the `test_report_html` directory under the program directory, and is saved as `mm-dd-yyyy.html`. In other words, an HTML report of a test run on January 1, 2008 would be stored as `01-01-2008.html`.

Examining the HTML File

Open the generated HTML file in a browser. It should look something like what is shown in Figure 6-1.

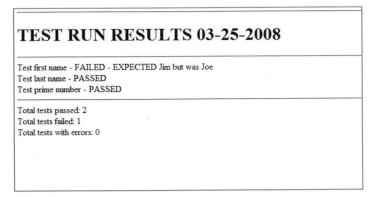

Figure 6-1

Press Enter to return to the main menu.

When Problems Occur

If for some reason the program cannot find the test run file, you will get an appropriate error message:

```
================================
GENERATE HTML REPORT
================================


    Enter the date of the test run in the
    following format: '01-01-2008'
    01-20-2008

        Problem opening test run file!

Press [Enter] to continue:
```

Press Enter to return to the main menu.

Displaying Product Help

If you type **5** and press Enter to display help, the following screen appears:

```
================================
TEST MANAGEMENT/REPORTING SYSTEM
================================
Welcome to the Test Management/Reporting system.
Using this program, you can run tests, list test
runs, show test results to the screen, and generate
HTML reports.

Press [Enter] to continue:
```

Press Enter to return to the main menu.

Design

No doubt familiar to you by now, this is a text-based, menu-driven program. It essentially runs and tests the data, and then outputs the results both to the screen and to an XML file. It then has options for querying the XML file for data and presenting it, or querying the XML file and then generating HTML from the query.

Modules

There are five modules in this application:

- ❑   test_manager.py is the main program, and it contains the menu that drives user interaction.
- ❑   test_run.py runs the tests and stores the results.
- ❑   test_list.py lists existing test runs.
- ❑   test_results.py shows results on the screen for any test run.
- ❑   test_html.py takes any existing test run as input and outputs the results to a formatted HTML page.

test_manager.py

test_manager.py is the module that a user actually loads. It contains the user menu and has one function. Table 6-1 shows the test_manager module function.

Table 6-1

Function	Return Type	Description
menu()	string	Presents a user menu. Takes the user selection and returns it to the caller.

test_run.py

test_run.py is the module that actually runs the tests, writes the results to an XML file, and outputs the results to the screen. It has four functions, described in Table 6-2.

Table 6-2

Function	Return Type	Description
test_firstname(fname)	string	Takes a first name as an argument, and then asks the user to enter a first name. If the names match, then the test passes; otherwise, the test fails. Test status is returned to the caller.
test_lastname(lname)	string	Takes a last name as an argument, and then asks the user to enter a last name. If the names match, then the test passes; otherwise, the test fails. Test status is returned to the caller.
test_prime_number()	string	Asks the user to enter a number. If the number entered is a prime number, then the test passes; otherwise, the test fails. Test status is returned to the caller.
run_tests()	none	Runs the tests (calling the above functions). Outputs results to an XML file and to the screen.

test_list.py

test_list.py lists, by date, all test runs. It has one function, described in Table 6-3.

Table 6-3

Function	Return Type	Description
list_tests()	none	Lists all test runs, based on the XML files stored in the test_runs subdirectory

test_results.py

test_results.py is the module that enables the user to enter a date corresponding to a completed test run, displaying the results of the test on the screen. It has one function, described in Table 6-4.

Table 6-4

Function	Return Type	Description
show_test_results()	none	Asks the user for a date corresponding to a completed test run, and then queries the XML file, extracting the results. Results are then formatted and output to the screen in a screen report.

test_html.py

`test_html` is the module that enables the user to enter a date corresponding to a completed test run, outputting the results to a formatted HTML file. It has one function, described in Table 6-5.

Table 6-5

Function	Return Type	Description
test_html_report()	none	Asks the user for a date corresponding to a completed test run, and then queries the XML file, extracting the results. Results are then formatted and output to an HTML file.

Code and Code Explanation

Essentially, this application uses XML files as a database of sorts. This is the strength of XML — it enables you to have structured information that can be queried without the overhead of a database. The following sections look at each code file, so you can see how the application is put together.

In the interests of page space, I've omitted the code headers, but make sure you use them. Your coworkers will thank you.

test_manager.py

The `test_manager` module is the program users actually run. It contains code that's run at the module level, and one function, `main()`:

```
import os, sys
import test_run, test_list, test_results, test_html

if sys.executable.find("exe") != -1:
    clearscreen = "cls"
    testpath = ".\\test_runs\\"
else:
    clearscreen = "clear"
    testpath = "./test_runs/"

#MAIN MENU
def menu():
    os.system(clearscreen)
    print """
```

(continued)

(continued)

```
    ==================================
    TEST MANAGEMENT/REPORTING SYSTEM
    ==================================
    1 - Run tests
    2 - List test runs
    3 - Show test results
    4 - Generate HTML test report
    5 - Help
    6 - Exit
    ==================================
    """
    choice = raw_input("Enter a choice and press enter: ")
    return choice

#TAKE CHOICE AND LAUNCH MODULE
choice = ""
while choice != "6":
    choice = menu()
    if choice == "1":
        os.system(clearscreen)
        test_run.run_tests(testpath)
    elif choice == "2":
        os.system(clearscreen)
        test_list.list_tests()
    elif choice == "3":
        os.system(clearscreen)
        test_results.show_test_results(testpath)
    elif choice == "4":
        os.system(clearscreen)
        test_html.test_html_report(testpath)
    elif choice == "5":
        os.system(clearscreen)
        print """
    ==================================
    TEST MANAGEMENT/REPORTING SYSTEM
    ==================================
    Welcome to the Test Management/Reporting system.
    Using this program, you can run tests, list test
    runs, show test results to the screen, and generate
    HTML reports.
    """
        raw_input("Press [Enter] to continue: ")
```

Main Program

Initially, the program imports modules that will be used:

```
import os, sys
import test_run, test_list, test_results, test_html
```

Notice that the user-created modules are on a different line than the standard modules (os and system). This is just to make the program more readable.

Just below the import statements is a block of code to initialize variables based on the operating system the user is running:

```
if sys.executable.find("exe") != -1:
    clearscreen = "cls"
    testpath = ".\\test_runs\\"
else:
    clearscreen = "clear"
    testpath = "./test_runs/"
```

Skipping over the menu() function for now, you can see the main program code:

```
#TAKE CHOICE AND LAUNCH MODULE
choice = ""
while choice != "6":
    choice = menu()
    if choice == "1":
        os.system(clearscreen)
        test_run.run_tests(testpath)
    elif choice == "2":
        os.system(clearscreen)
        test_list.list_tests()
    elif choice == "3":
        os.system(clearscreen)
        test_results.show_test_results(testpath)
    elif choice == "4":
        os.system(clearscreen)
        test_html.test_html_report(testpath)
    elif choice == "5":
        os.system(clearscreen)
        print """
================================
TEST MANAGEMENT/REPORTING SYSTEM
================================
Welcome to the Test Management/Reporting system.
Using this program, you can run tests, list test
runs, show test results to the screen, and generate
HTML reports.
        """
        raw_input("Press [Enter] to continue: ")
```

As in previous programs, you initialize the `choice` variable, and then use a `while` loop to call the `menu()` function and assign the return value to the variable `choice`:

```
choice = ""
while choice != "6":
    choice = menu()
```

You then use an `if-elif` construct to perform different operations based on what the user entered (and what was assigned to the `choice` variable):

```
choice = ""
while choice != "6":
    choice = menu()
    if choice == "1":
        os.system(clearscreen)
        test_run.run_tests(testpath)
    elif choice == "2":
        os.system(clearscreen)
        test_list.list_tests()
    elif choice == "3":
        os.system(clearscreen)
        test_results.show_test_results(testpath)
    elif choice == "4":
        os.system(clearscreen)
        test_html.test_html_report(testpath)
    elif choice == "5":
        os.system(clearscreen)
        print """
================================
TEST MANAGEMENT/REPORTING SYSTEM
================================
Welcome to the Test Management/Reporting system.
Using this program, you can run tests, list test
runs, show test results to the screen, and generate
HTML reports.
        """
        raw_input("Press [Enter] to continue: ")
```

If the user enters **6**, then execution falls through the end of the `if` statement, and the program terminates.

menu()

The menu() function displays a user menu, takes a user selection, and returns that choice to the caller:

```
def menu():
    os.system('cls')
    print """
    =================================
    TEST MANAGEMENT/REPORTING SYSTEM
    =================================
    1 - Run tests
    2 - List test runs
    3 - Show test results
    4 - Generate HTML test report
    5 - Help
    6 - Exit
    =================================
    """
    choice = raw_input("Enter a choice and press enter: ")
    return choice
```

As shown in the preceding code, this function first clears the screen:

```
os.system(clarscreen)
```

After that, a menu is displayed:

```
print """
=================================
TEST MANAGEMENT/REPORTING SYSTEM
=================================
1 - Run tests
2 - List test runs
3 - Show test results
4 - Generate HTML test report
5 - Help
6 - Exit
=================================
"""
```

Finally, the user's selection is assigned to a variable, whose value is returned to the caller:

```
choice = raw_input("Enter a choice and press enter: ")
return choice
```

test_run.py

The `test_run.py` module is responsible for running tests, displaying the results on the screen, and creating the XML test run file. It is the longest, most complex module in the application:

```python
import datetime, math

def test_firstname(fname):
    fname_input = raw_input("\tEnter your first name: ")
    if fname_input == fname:
        return "PASSED"
    else:
        return "FAILED - EXPECTED " + fname + " but was " + fname_input

def test_lastname(lname):
    lname_input = raw_input("\tEnter your last name: ")
    if lname_input == lname:
        return "PASSED"
    else:
        return "FAILED - EXPECTED " + lname + " but was " + lname_input

def test_prime_number():
    primes = [2, 3, 5, 7, 11, 13, 17, 19, 23, 29, 31, 37, 41, 43, 47, \
              53, 59, 61, 67, 71, 73, 79, 83, 89, 97]
    num = raw_input("\tPrime number test - enter a number from 1 to 99: ")
    number = int(num)
    if number in primes:
        return "PASSED"
    else:
        return "FAILED - " + str(number) + " is not a prime number 1 to 99"

def run_tests():

    def testcount(test_results):
    #Compile test results and return them in a list
        tests_passed = 0
        tests_failed = 0
        tests_error = 0
        for test_result in test_results:
            if test_result == "PASSED":
                tests_passed += 1
            elif test_result[0:6] == "FAILED":
                tests_failed += 1
            else:
                tests_error += 1
        results = [tests_passed, tests_failed, tests_error]
        return results
```

```
#Run tests
print """
================================
RUN TESTS
================================
"""
result_firstname = test_firstname("Jim")
result_lastname = test_lastname("Knowlton")
result_prime_number = test_prime_number()
total_results = [result_firstname, result_lastname, result_prime_number]
results = testcount(total_results)

#Output test results to screen
print """
================================
TEST RUN RESULTS
================================
Test first name - %s
Test last name - %s
Test prime number - %s
================================
Total tests passed:  %i
Total tests failed:  %i
Total tests with errors:  %i
""" % (result_firstname, result_lastname, result_prime_number, \
results[0], results[1], results[2])

#Format XML output for test run
test_output_xml = """<testresult>
<testfirstname>%s</testfirstname>
<testlastname>%s</testlastname>
<testprimenumber>%s</testprimenumber>
<testspassed>%i</testspassed>
<testsfailed>%i</testsfailed>
<testserror>%i</testserror>
</testresult>""" % \
(result_firstname, result_lastname, result_prime_number, \
    results[0], results[1], results[2])

today = datetime.datetime.now().strftime("%m-%d-%Y")
output_filename = ".\\test_runs\\" + today + ".xml"
test_output = open(output_filename, 'w')
test_output.write(test_output_xml)
test_output.close()
raw_input("Press [Enter] to continue: ")
```

Whew! Yes, there's a lot going on. Let's look at this module function by function.

test_firstname(fname)

The first three functions are the tests. Let's look at the first of them:

```
def test_firstname(fname):
    fname_input = raw_input("\tEnter your first name: ")
    if fname_input == fname:
        return "PASSED"
    else:
        return "FAILED - EXPECTED " + fname + " but was " + fname_input
```

This function simply takes a string parameter `fname`. It prompts the user to enter a first name and assigns the result to a string variable:

```
fname_input = raw_input("\tEnter your first name: ")
```

It then compares what the user has entered to the string passed as a parameter. If they match, then the string `"PASSED"` is returned; otherwise, a failure string is returned:

```
if fname_input == fname:
    return "PASSED"
else:
    return "FAILED - EXPECTED " + fname + " but was " + fname_input
```

test_lastname(lname)

The second test function looks very similar:

```
def test_lastname(lname):
    lname_input = raw_input("\tEnter your last name: ")
    if lname_input == lname:
        return "PASSED"
    else:
        return "FAILED - EXPECTED " + lname + " but was " + lname_input
```

This function simply takes a string parameter `lname`. It prompts the user to enter a last name and assigns the result to a string variable:

```
lname_input = raw_input("\tEnter your last name: ")
```

It then compares what the user has entered to the string passed as a parameter. If they match, then the string `"PASSED"` is returned; otherwise, a failure string is returned:

```
if lname_input == lname:
    return "PASSED"
else:
    return "FAILED - EXPECTED " + lname + " but was " + lname_input
```

test_prime_number()

The final test function determines whether a number is a prime number:

```python
def test_prime_number():
    primes = [2, 3, 5, 7, 11, 13, 17, 19, 23, 29, 31, 37, 41, 43, 47, \
              53, 59, 61, 67, 71, 73, 79, 83, 89, 97]
    num = raw_input("\tPrime number test - enter a number from 1 to 99: ")
    number = int(num)
    if number in primes:
        return "PASSED"
    else:
        return "FAILED - " + str(number) + " is not a prime number 1 to 99"
```

First, it initializes a list comprising all the prime numbers less than 100. Then it prompts the user to enter a number, assigns the number to a variable, and converts the string entered to its integer equivalent:

```python
num = raw_input("\tPrime number test - enter a number from 1 to 99: ")
number = int(num)
```

The next block of code tests the number to determine whether it is in the list. If it is, then it returns a "PASSED" string; otherwise, it returns a failure string:

```python
    if number in primes:
        return "PASSED"
    else:
        return "FAILED - " + str(number) + " is not a prime number 1 to 99"
```

run_tests()

Although this function shows up last in the module sequentially, it drives everything else:

```python
def run_tests(testpath):

    def testcount(test_results):
    #Compile test results and return them in a list
        tests_passed = 0
        tests_failed = 0
        tests_error = 0
        for test_result in test_results:
            if test_result == "PASSED":
                tests_passed += 1
            elif test_result[0:6] == "FAILED":
                tests_failed += 1
            else:
                tests_error += 1
        results = [tests_passed, tests_failed, tests_error]
        return results
```

(continued)

(continued)

```
        #Run tests
        print """
        ===============================
        RUN TESTS
        ===============================
        """
        result_firstname = test_firstname("Jim")
        result_lastname = test_lastname("Knowlton")
        result_prime_number = test_prime_number()
        total_results = [result_firstname, result_lastname, result_prime_number]
        results = testcount(total_results)

        #Output test results to screen
        print """
        ===============================
        TEST RUN RESULTS
        ===============================
        Test first name - %s
        Test last name - %s
        Test prime number - %s
        ===============================
        Total tests passed:  %i
        Total tests failed:  %i
        Total tests with errors:  %i
        """ % (result_firstname, result_lastname, result_prime_number, \
        results[0], results[1], results[2])

        #Format XML output for test run
        test_output_xml = """<testresult>
        <testfirstname>%s</testfirstname>
        <testlastname>%s</testlastname>
        <testprimenumber>%s</testprimenumber>
        <testspassed>%i</testspassed>
        <testsfailed>%i</testsfailed>
        <testserror>%i</testserror>
        </testresult>""" % \
        (result_firstname, result_lastname, result_prime_number, \
            results[0], results[1], results[2])

        today = datetime.datetime.now().strftime("%m-%d-%Y")
        output_filename = testpath + today + ".xml"
try:
        test_output = open(output_filename, "w")
        test_output.write(test_output_xml)
        test_output.close()
    except:
        print "Problem writing to file!"
        raw_input("Press [Enter] to continue: ")
```

We'll skip over the `testcount()` function for now, returning to it in a minute.

The first bit of code inside the function displays a menu banner:

```
print """
================================
RUN TESTS
================================
"""
```

Notice that the first block of code is a nested function. A nice feature of Python is that functions can be nested, enabling you to provide a service to just the functions they are nested inside of.

The next three lines of code actually call the test functions and assign the results to variables:

```
result_firstname = test_firstname("Jim")
result_lastname = test_lastname("Knowlton")
result_prime_number = test_prime_number()
```

As you can see, I set the correct answers for the first two tests to correspond with my name (naturally). Feel free to change them to your name — or anything else you choose, for that matter.

The next line creates an array with the results for each test that has been run:

```
total_results = [result_firstname, result_lastname, result_prime_number]
```

Then, the `testcount()` function is called, which returns a list containing the cumulative count of passed, failed, and error tests. (We'll look more at that function in a minute). The cumulative counts are assigned to variable results:

```
results = testcount(total_results)
```

The next step is to output the results to the screen, in a readable format:

```
#Output test results to screen
print """
================================
TEST RUN RESULTS
================================
Test first name - %s
Test last name - %s
Test prime number - %s
================================
Total tests passed:  %i
Total tests failed:  %i
Total tests with errors:  %i
""" % (result_firstname, result_lastname, result_prime_number, \
results[0], results[1], results[2])
```

Next, the program needs to write the results to an XML file. First, the program creates a string variable and populates it with the XML text to go in the file:

```
test_output_xml = """<testresult>
<testfirstname>%s</testfirstname>
<testlastname>%s</testlastname>
<testprimenumber>%s</testprimenumber>
<testspassed>%i</testspassed>
<testsfailed>%i</testsfailed>
<testserror>%i</testserror>
</testresult>""" % \
(result_firstname, result_lastname, result_prime_number, \
    results[0], results[1], results[2])
```

Because the filename is based on the date, the next step is to get the system date and then format a string that will be the name of the file:

```
today = datetime.datetime.now().strftime("%m-%d-%Y")
output_filename = testpath + today + ".xml"
```

Finally, the file is opened, written to using the formatted string (with the XML code), and closed:

```
try:
    test_output = open(output_filename, "w")
    test_output.write(test_output_xml)
    test_output.close()
except:
    print "Problem writing to file!"
```

testcount()

The testcount() function, which is nested inside of test_run(), takes a list of test results and counts the number of passed, failed, and error tests:

```
def testcount(test_results):
    #Compile test results and return them in a list
        tests_passed = 0
        tests_failed = 0
        tests_error = 0
        for test_result in test_results:
            if test_result == "PASSED":
                tests_passed += 1
            elif test_result[0:6] == "FAILED":
                tests_failed += 1
            else:
                tests_error += 1
        results = [tests_passed, tests_failed, tests_error]
        return results
```

The function first initializes the variables for passed, failed, and error tests to zero:

```
tests_passed = 0
tests_failed = 0
tests_error = 0
```

Following that, the function implements a `for` loop, which iterates through all the results and increments the count of each category based on the respective results found:

```
for test_result in test_results:
    if test_result == "PASSED":
        tests_passed += 1
    elif test_result[0:6] == "FAILED":
        tests_failed += 1
    else:
        tests_error += 1
```

Finally, the results are compiled into a list and returned to the caller:

```
results = [tests_passed, tests_failed, tests_error]
return results
```

test_list.py

The `test_list.py` module lists all test runs by simply parsing a directory listing of test run files.

list_tests()

`list_tests()` is the only function in the module:

```
import os, glob

def list_tests():
    os.chdir("test_runs")
    filelist = glob.glob("*.xml")

    print """
===============================
LIST TEST RUNS
===============================
"""
    for f in filelist:
        item = f.strip('.xml')
        print "\t" + item
    print """
===============================
"""
    raw_input("Press [Enter] to continue: ")
```

The function starts by changing the current directory to the directory where the test run files are located:

```
os.chdir("test_runs")
```

Then it uses the `glob` module to assign to the list `filelist` all XML files in the directory:

```
filelist = glob.glob("*.xml")
```

The next step is to print the menu item banner:

```
print """
==================================
LIST TEST RUNS
==================================
"""
```

To print the list of test runs, a `for` loop is used to iterate through the list that was created. The `strip` string method is used to strip out the .xml extension from each file, so that it just shows a date for each item:

```
for f in filelist:
    item = f.strip('.xml')
    print "\t" + item
```

Finally, the bottom bar of the banner is displayed on the screen:

```
print """
==================================
"""
```

test_results.py

The `test_results.py` module enables a user to enter a date corresponding to a test run and retrieve the results from the XML file and display them on the screen:

```
from xml.dom import minidom
import time

def show_test_results(testpath):

    print """
    ==================================
    SHOW TEST RESULTS
    ==================================
    """
```

```
prompt = """
Enter the date of the test run in the
following format: '01-01-2008'
(or type 'today' for today)
"""
test_date = raw_input (prompt)
if test_date == "today":
    test_date == datetime.datetime.now().strftime("%m-%d-%Y")

test_run_file = testpath + test_date + ".xml"

#Get nodes from XML document
try:
    test_run = minidom.parse(test_run_file)
except:
    print "\n\tProblem opening test run file!\n"
    raw_input("Press [Enter] to continue: ")
    return

test_result_node = test_run.childNodes[0]
test_firstname_node = test_result_node.childNodes[1]
test_lastname_node = test_result_node.childNodes[3]
test_prime_node = test_result_node.childNodes[5]
test_passed_node = test_result_node.childNodes[7]
test_failed_node = test_result_node.childNodes[9]
test_error_node = test_result_node.childNodes[11]

#Get text from relevant nodes
test_firstname_result = test_firstname_node.firstChild.data
test_lastname_result = test_lastname_node.firstChild.data
test_prime_result = test_prime_node.firstChild.data
test_passed_result = test_passed_node.firstChild.data
test_failed_result = test_failed_node.firstChild.data
test_error_result = test_error_node.firstChild.data

#Produce result to screen
print """
================================
TEST RUN RESULTS %s
================================
Test first name - %s
Test last name - %s
Test prime number - %s
================================
Total tests passed:  %s
Total tests failed:  %s
Total tests with errors:  %s
""" % (test_date, test_firstname_result, test_lastname_result, \
test_prime_result, test_passed_result, test_failed_result, \
test_error_result)

raw_input("Press [Enter] to continue: ")
```

show_test_results()

This function starts out by displaying the menu item banner:

```
print """
=================================
SHOW TEST RESULTS
=================================
"""
```

Then the user is prompted to enter a date corresponding to a test run, and the user's entry is assigned to a variable:

```
prompt = """
Enter the date of the test run in the
following format: '01-01-2008'
"""
test_date = raw_input (prompt)
```

A variable is then created for the path and name of the XML file:

```
test_run_file = testpath + test_date + ".xml"
```

Next, it is time to open the XML file and parse it, using the `minidom` module:

```
#Get nodes from XML document
try:
    test_run = minidom.parse(test_run_file)
except:
    print "\n\tProblem opening test run file!\n"
    raw_input("Press [Enter] to continue: ")
    return
```

Notice that the opening of the file is enclosed in a `try`/`except` block, just in case there is a problem, such as the file not being found.

The next step is to use the node stored in the `test_run` variable and create variables corresponding to all the nodes from which we need to extract data:

```
test_result_node = test_run.childNodes[0]
test_firstname_node = test_result_node.childNodes[1]
test_lastname_node = test_result_node.childNodes[3]
test_prime_node = test_result_node.childNodes[5]
test_passed_node = test_result_node.childNodes[7]
test_failed_node = test_result_node.childNodes[9]
test_error_node = test_result_node.childNodes[11]
```

Once the nodes are assigned to variables, the data from those nodes can be extracted and assigned to variables:

```
#Get text from relevant nodes
test_firstname_result = test_firstname_node.firstChild.data
test_lastname_result = test_lastname_node.firstChild.data
test_prime_result = test_prime_node.firstChild.data
test_passed_result = test_passed_node.firstChild.data
test_failed_result = test_failed_node.firstChild.data
test_error_result = test_error_node.firstChild.data
```

Finally, the test results for the retrieved XML file can be displayed on the screen:

```
#Produce result to screen
print """
===============================
TEST RUN RESULTS %s
===============================
Test first name - %s
Test last name - %s
Test prime number - %s
===============================
Total tests passed:  %s
Total tests failed:  %s
Total tests with errors:  %s
""" % (test_date, test_firstname_result, test_lastname_result, \
test_prime_result, test_passed_result, test_failed_result, \
test_error_result)
```

test_html.py

The `test_html.py` module enables a user to enter a date corresponding to a test run, and generates an HTML report that can be viewed in a web browser:

```
from xml.dom import minidom

def test_html_report(testpath):
    print """
    ===============================
    GENERATE HTML REPORT
    ===============================
    """
    prompt = """
    Enter the date of the test run in the
    following format: '01-01-2008'
    """
    test_date = raw_input (prompt)

    test_run_file = testpath + test_date + ".xml"
```

(continued)

(continued)

```python
#Get nodes from XML document
try:
    test_run = minidom.parse(test_run_file)
except:
    print "\n\tProblem opening test run file!\n"
    raw_input("Press [Enter] to continue: ")
    return
test_result_node = test_run.childNodes[0]
test_firstname_node = test_result_node.childNodes[1]
test_lastname_node = test_result_node.childNodes[3]
test_prime_node = test_result_node.childNodes[5]
test_passed_node = test_result_node.childNodes[7]
test_failed_node = test_result_node.childNodes[9]
test_error_node = test_result_node.childNodes[11]

#Get text from relevant nodes
test_firstname_result = test_firstname_node.firstChild.data
test_lastname_result = test_lastname_node.firstChild.data
test_prime_result = test_prime_node.firstChild.data
test_passed_result = test_passed_node.firstChild.data
test_failed_result = test_failed_node.firstChild.data
test_error_result = test_error_node.firstChild.data

#Produce result to html
html_output = """
<HTML>
<TITLE>Test Report - %s</TITLE>
<HR>
<H1>TEST RUN RESULTS %s</H1>
<HR>
<BODY>
Test first name - %s<br>
Test last name - %s<br>
Test prime number - %s<br>
<HR>
Total tests passed:  %s<br>
Total tests failed:  %s<br>
Total tests with errors:  %s<br>
</BODY>
</HTML>
""" % (test_date, test_date, test_firstname_result, test_lastname_result, \
test_prime_result, test_passed_result, test_failed_result, test_error_result)

filename = os.path.join(os.curdir, 'test_report_html', test_date + ".html")
output_file = open(filename, 'w')
output_file.write(html_output)
output_file.close()

print "\n\t-- HTML Report Generated --"
raw_input("\tPress [Enter] to continue: ")
```

test_html_report ()

This function starts out by displaying the menu item banner:

```
print """
=================================
GENERATE HTML REPORT
=================================
"""
```

The user is prompted to enter the date associated with a test run, in the appropriate format:

```
prompt = """
Enter the date of the test run in the
following format: '01-01-2008'
"""
test_date = raw_input (prompt)
```

The function then has a line of code to construct a string variable with the date input above, adding the path to the test run files and the .XML extension:

```
test_run_file = testpath + test_date + ".xml"
```

The XML test run file is then opened and parsed, using the `minidom` module:

```
#Get nodes from XML document
try:
    test_run = minidom.parse(test_run_file)
except:
    print "\n\tProblem opening test run file!\n"
    raw_input("Press [Enter] to continue: ")
    return
```

Variables associated with all the nodes to be accessed are then created:

```
test_result_node = test_run.childNodes[0]
test_firstname_node = test_result_node.childNodes[1]
test_lastname_node = test_result_node.childNodes[3]
test_prime_node = test_result_node.childNodes[5]
test_passed_node = test_result_node.childNodes[7]
test_failed_node = test_result_node.childNodes[9]
test_error_node = test_result_node.childNodes[11]
```

With the nodes assigned to variables, the data can be extracted from the nodes and assigned to variables:

```
#Get text from relevant nodes
test_firstname_result = test_firstname_node.firstChild.data
test_lastname_result = test_lastname_node.firstChild.data
test_prime_result = test_prime_node.firstChild.data
test_passed_result = test_passed_node.firstChild.data
test_failed_result = test_failed_node.firstChild.data
test_error_result = test_error_node.firstChild.data
```

After all the needed data from the XML file is assigned to variables, the HTML text can be constructed:

```
html_output = """
    <HTML>
    <TITLE>Test Report - %s</TITLE>
    <HR>
    <H1>TEST RUN RESULTS %s</H1>
    <HR>
    <BODY>
    Test first name - %s<br>
    Test last name - %s<br>
    Test prime number - %s<br>
    <HR>
    Total tests passed:  %s<br>
    Total tests failed:  %s<br>
    Total tests with errors:  %s<br>
    </BODY>
    </HTML>
    """ % (test_date, test_date, test_firstname_result, test_lastname_result, \
    test_prime_result, test_passed_result, test_failed_result, test_error_result)
```

The next bit of code is to open the HTML file for writing, and then write the HTML to the file:

```
filename = os.path.join(os.curdir, 'test_report_html', test_date + ".html")
output_file = open(filename, 'w')
output_file.write(html_output)
output_file.close()
```

Finally, a status message is displayed, letting the user know that the HTML file has been created:

```
print "\n\t-- HTML Report Generated --"
```

Testing

There are several "moving parts" with this application, so there are several potential areas for testing:

❏ The tests in this application are fairly simple and trivial. You could expand on the test suite by testing a "real" application, and see what issues or problems arise. This framework could even be used with the Python `unittest` module, which is covered in Chapter 10.

❏ Examine the XML files that are being created, to verify that the format of the files is consistent and expected.

❏ Create a suite with a large number of tests (which would create a large XML file). Are there any issues with the `minidom` parser when working with large files?

Modifying the Program

There are several ways this project could be enhanced, including the following:

❏ Currently, the application saves test data by date, such that multiple runs on one day overwrite each other. You could change this behavior by having the files use a date-time stamp.

❏ You could have an option to look at "test history," which takes the name of a test as input and then goes through each test run and produces a report of each result, based on the date.

❏ You could create command-line arguments so that, for example, if you just want to execute a test run and don't want to have to see the menu, you can do that.

Summary

In this chapter you learned how to build your own "homegrown" framework for testing software, but more important, you learned how to work with XML files, which are a great resource to use as a lightweight source for structured, persistent data. Specifically, you learned how to do the following:

❏ Create XML documents based on input from the user

❏ Query XML documents using the `minidom` module

❏ Create HTML from XML data

More About the Minidom Module

Here are some more interesting things to know about the `minidom` module:

❑   It supports both byte and Unicode strings, making it useful if your application needs to support multiple languages.

❑   It can also be used to access and manipulate XHTML documents.

❑   There is a `parseString()` function that enables you to take an XML string (not from a file) and parse it; this is very useful if you have two programs that are communicating through XML.

7

Version Management System

Imagine you are the administrator of three computer labs. Some of the machines have had their versions of Java and Python updated, but you're not sure how many, or which ones. You *could* go to each computer individually and check.

But you're not going to do that.

By building a Python script to connect to your machines and check version levels, you can automatically build a list of the version of installed applications on each computer.

The version management system in this chapter shows how you can use Telnet to retrieve version information for a list of applications (in this program, the applications checked will be Java, Python, and Perl). The program will then write the results of the check to a CSV log file.

The application will perform the following functions:

❏   Allow the user to identify an IP address and a list of applications to check for (entered via command-line arguments)

❏   Log in, using Telnet, to the machine and check the version numbers of each application

❏   Write the results of the query to a CSV log file

What Is Telnet?

Telnet is an Internet protocol used on Internet or Local Area Network (LAN) networks. Basically, Telnet enables you to log on to remote systems to perform various tasks. Python has a `telnetlib` module that enables a script to emulate a Telnet client. That is how the program in this chapter will get application version information about each remote computer.

Using the Program

Before the program is run, any remote computers to be connected to from the application must be set up.

The computers connected to in this application were Linux machines, but the application could easily be adapted to also connect to Windows machines.

Setting Up Remote Computers

Remote computers need to have the following features enabled:

1. Java, Python, and Perl should be installed.

2. A Telnet server should be installed and running (the application assumes it is running on its default port).

3. A common account (with a common password) should be set for each machine.

Important Security Note!

In this application, we are creating an account with the same user and password for every machine in the system. This is not a good security practice in real life. Check out the end of the chapter for some suggested security enhancements.

Running the Program — Command-Line Syntax

You can get to the program by navigating to the directory corresponding to this chapter. Once again, the files are available for download from the website (www.wrox.com). To run the application, simply go to a command prompt, and from the directory on your system where the Chapter 7 program files are located, type the following:

```
python version_checker.py <ip address> <applications>
```

The command-line options are as follows:

❑   <ip address> — Enter the IP address to connect to.

❑   <applications> — Enter the applications, enclosed in quotes. The applications can be selected from the following:

   ❑   Java

   ❑   Python

   ❑   Perl

Command-Line Examples

If the following is typed at the command line, the script will connect to IP address 192.168.1.108 and check the versions of Java, Python, and Perl:

```
python version_checker.py 192.168.1.108 "java python perl"
```

The result will look something like this:

```
I:\Applied_Python\Chapter_7>python version_checker.py 192.168.1.108 "java python
 perl"
HOST - 192.168.1.108
Java version = 1.6.0_0
Python version = 2.5.1
Perl version = 5.8.8
```

If the following is typed at the command line, the script will connect to IP address 192.168.1.108 and check the versions of Java and Perl:

```
python version_checker.py 192.168.1.108 "java perl"
```

The result will look something like this:

```
I:\Applied_Python\Chapter_7>python version_checker.py 192.168.1.108 "java perl"
HOST - 192.168.1.108
Java version = 1.6.0_0
Perl version = 5.8.8
```

If the following is typed at the command line, the script will connect to IP address 192.168.1.108 and check the versions of Perl and Python:

```
python version_checker.py 192.168.1.108 "perl python"
```

Notice that the order of the applications listed does not matter. The result will look something like this:

```
I:\Applied_Python\Chapter_7>python version_checker.py 192.168.1.108 "perl python"
HOST -  192.168.1.108

Python version =  2.5.1
Perl version =  5.8.8
```

If the following is typed at the command line, the script will connect to IP address 192.168.1.108 and check the version of Perl:

```
python version_checker.py 192.168.1.108 "perl"
```

The result will look something like this:

```
I:\Applied_Python\Chapter_7>python version_checker.py 192.168.1.108 " perl"
HOST -  192.168.1.108
Perl version =  5.8.8
```

If you don't enter all the options, a message like the following one will be displayed:

```
I:\Applied_Python\Chapter_7>python version_checker.py 192.168.1.108
 Insufficient arguments:  suggested use -
   python version_checker.py <ip address> "<applications to check>"

   NOTES:
   1.  Replace <ip address> with the ip address you want to check.
   2.  Replace <applications to check> with any combination of the following
       applications (in quotes):
           java
           python
           perl

   EXAMPLE:

   python version_checker.py 1.1.1.1 "python java"

   This command will check the versions of Python and Java on computer with
ip address 1.1.1.1.
```

Viewing the CSV Log File

After you have run a few reports, you can view the CSV log of the version checks. If you open the CSV file in a spreadsheet program, it will look something like what is shown in Figure 7-1.

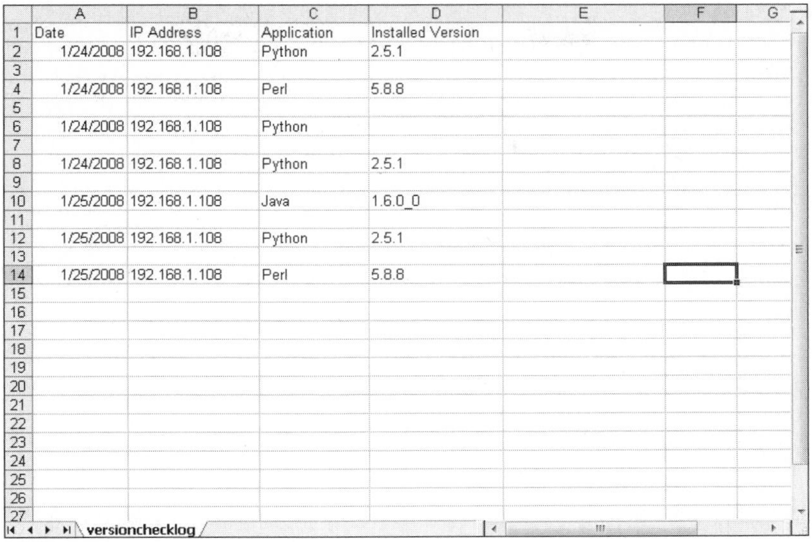

Date	IP Address	Application	Installed Version
1/24/2008	192.168.1.108	Python	2.5.1
1/24/2008	192.168.1.108	Perl	5.8.8
1/24/2008	192.168.1.108	Python	
1/24/2008	192.168.1.108	Python	2.5.1
1/25/2008	192.168.1.108	Java	1.6.0_0
1/25/2008	192.168.1.108	Python	2.5.1
1/25/2008	192.168.1.108	Perl	5.8.8

versionchecklog

Figure 7-1

Running Against Several Different Machines in Batch Mode

To run the script against several different machines in batch mode, you could simply create a shell script (or batch file, if on Windows) that runs the script against several different machines, as in the following example:

```
python version_checker.py 192.168.1.108 "java python perl"
python version_checker.py 192.168.1.109 "java perl"
python version_checker.py 192.168.1.110 "java python perl"
python version_checker.py 192.168.1.111 "python perl"
python version_checker.py 192.168.1.112 "python"
python version_checker.py 192.168.1.113 "perl python"
python version_checker.py 192.168.1.114 "java"
python version_checker.py 192.168.1.115 "perl"
python version_checker.py 192.168.1.116 "java python perl"
python version_checker.py 192.168.1.117 "java perl"
python version_checker.py 192.168.1.118 "python perl"
python version_checker.py 192.168.1.119 "perl"
python version_checker.py 192.168.1.120 "java python perl"
python version_checker.py 192.168.1.121 "java perl"
python version_checker.py 192.168.1.122 "python"
python version_checker.py 192.168.1.123 "java python perl"
```

Design

This is the first application that doesn't have any kind of a "driveable" user interface — it uses the command line to pass options to the script. This enables a script to be more easily implemented in another script or batch file, which is why it was handled this way in this case.

Modules

There are three modules in this application:

❏ version_checker.py is the main program. It receives the command-line option, prints error messages, and calls functions in other modules to do the checking and output to the CSV file.

❏ check_versions.py logs in to the remote machine and returns the version of the particular application being checked.

❏ csv_report.py takes a version check result and writes it to the CSV log file.

version_checker.py

version_checker.py is the main program. It calls the functions to run checks and output the results to a CSV. It also displays output to the screen. Table 7-1 shows the version_checker module functions.

Table 7-1

Function	Return Type	Description
check_arguments()	none	Checks arguments entered at the command line. If there are insufficient arguments, then it generates an error message and exits.
get_versions ()	none	Launches functions to log in to the remote computer to display and log results.

check_versions.py

check_versions.py is called by version_checker.py and checks versions of the respective applications being checked. Table 7-2 shows the check_versions module functions.

Table 7-2

Function	Return Type	Description
check_java(host, user, password)	string	Takes hostname, username, and password as arguments, connects to the host, checks the version of Java, and returns that version to the caller
check_python(host, user, password)	string	Takes hostname, username, and password as arguments, connects to the host, checks the version of Python, and returns that version to the caller
check_perl(host, user, password)	string	Takes hostname, username, and password as arguments, connects to the host, checks the version of Perl, and returns that version to the caller

csv_report.py

csv_report.py takes the results of a version check and outputs the results to the CSV report log. Table 7-3 shows the csv_report module function.

Table 7-3

Function	Return Type	Description
write_csv_log(host, application, version)	none	Takes host, application, and version information as parameters and outputs an entry to the CSV log file

Code and Code Explanation

Essentially, this application takes parameters at the command line, logs in (through Telnet) to a remote computer, checks the version of an identified application, and reports the result to the screen and to a CSV log file.

In the interests of page space, I've omitted the code headers, but make sure you use them. Your coworkers will thank you.

version_checker.py

The `version_checker` module is the program users actually run on the command line. It contains code that's run at the module level, and two functions:

```python
import sys
import check_versions, csv_report

HOST = sys.argv[1]
USER = "jars"
PASSWORD = "jars"

def check_arguments():
    if (len(sys.argv)) < 3:
        print """ Insufficient arguments:  suggested use -
        python version_checker.py <ip address> "<applications to check>"

        NOTES:
        1.  Replace <ip address> with the ip address you want to check.
        2.  Replace <applications to check> with any combination of the following
applications (in quotes):
                java
                python
                perl

        EXAMPLE:

        python version_checker.py 1.1.1.1 "python java"

        This command will check the versions of Python and Java on computer with ip
address 1.1.1.1."""
        sys.exit()


def get_versions():
    print "HOST - ", HOST
    if "java" in sys.argv[2]:
        java_version = check_versions.check_java(HOST, USER, PASSWORD)
        csv_report.write_csv_log(HOST, "Java", java_version)
        print "Java version = ", java_version
    if "python" in sys.argv[2]:
        python_version = check_versions.check_python(HOST, USER, PASSWORD)
        csv_report.write_csv_log(HOST, "Python", python_version)
        print "Python version = ", python_version
    if "perl" in sys.argv[2]:
        perl_version = check_versions.check_perl(HOST, USER, PASSWORD)
        csv_report.write_csv_log(HOST, "Perl", perl_version)
        print "Perl version = ", perl_version

check_arguments()
get_versions()
```

Main Program

The main program starts off by importing the modules it needs:

```
import sys
import check_versions, csv_report
```

Then variables are initialized for the host, user, and password:

```
HOST = sys.argv[1]
USER = "jars"
PASSWORD = "jars"
```

Note two things about the preceding code:

❑   The variable HOST is assigned the first command-line parameter. This is how Python enables a program to take command-line arguments and use them in a Python script.

❑   The user and password are assigned here. If you want the password to be something different, change it here.

Down at the bottom of the module (after the function definitions), the program runs the functions to check both the arguments and the versions:

```
check_arguments()
get_versions()
```

check_arguments()

check_arguments() checks the command-line arguments entered at the command line to ensure that the correct number of arguments appears. If not, it generates an error and exits:

```
def check_arguments():
    if len(sys.argv) < 3:
        print """ Insufficient arguments:  suggested use -
        python version_checker.py <ip address> "<applications to check>"

        NOTES:
        1.  Replace <ip address> with the ip address you want to check.
        2.  Replace <applications to check> with any combination of the
following applications (in quotes):
                java
                python
                perl

        EXAMPLE:
```

(continued)

(continued)

```
        python version_checker.py 1.1.1.1 "python java"

        This command will check the versions of Python and Java on computer with
  ip address 1.1.1.1."""
        sys.exit()
```

The function initially determines whether two arguments appear (the first argument is the Python script name, so there should be three elements in `sys.argv`):

```
  if len(sys.argv) < 3:
```

If there are fewer than two command-line arguments, it prints an error/help message:

```
        print """ Insufficient arguments:  suggested use -
        python version_checker.py <ip address> "<applications to check>"

        NOTES:
        1.  Replace <ip address> with the ip address you want to check.
        2.  Replace <applications to check> with any combination of the following
  applications (in quotes):
                java
                python
                perl

        EXAMPLE:

        python version_checker.py 1.1.1.1 "python java"

        This command will check the versions of Python and Java on computer with ip
  address 1.1.1.1."""
```

The last line of the `if` loop (and the function) is a command to exit:

```
        sys.exit(1)
```

> **Notice that you exit with a 1. Non-zero exit codes are for situations in which something has gone wrong, so if you exit the program in an error condition, it makes sense to pass a 1.**

get_versions()

The `get_versions()` function launches the various functions to check the application version, based on what the user entered on the command line:

```
def get_versions():
    print "HOST - ", HOST
    if sys.argv[2].find("java") != -1:
        java_version = check_versions.check_java(HOST, USER, PASSWORD)
        csv_report.write_csv_log(HOST, "Java", java_version)
        print "Java version = ", java_version
    if sys.argv[2].find("python") != -1:
        python_version = check_versions.check_python(HOST, USER, PASSWORD)
        csv_report.write_csv_log(HOST, "Python", python_version)
        print "Python version = ", python_version
    if sys.argv[2].find("perl") != -1:
        perl_version = check_versions.check_perl(HOST, USER, PASSWORD)
        csv_report.write_csv_log(HOST, "Perl", perl_version)
        print "Perl version = ", perl_version
```

The first thing the function does is print a header with the IP address of the entered host:

```
print "HOST - ", HOST
```

Then the function implements an `if` block to determine whether "java" was entered on the command line. If it was, then the `check_java()` function is called and the result is assigned to the variable `java_version`:

```
java_version = check_versions.check_java(HOST, USER, PASSWORD)
```

Then the `write_csv_log()` function is called to write the result to the CSV log file:

```
csv_report.write_csv_log(HOST, "Java", java_version)
```

The `if` block ends by printing the result to the screen:

```
print "Java version = ", java_version
```

Then the function implements an `if` block to determine whether "python" was entered on the command line. If it was, then the `check_python()` function is called and the result is assigned to the variable `python_version`:

```
python_version = check_versions.check_python(HOST, USER, PASSWORD)
```

Then the `write_csv_log()` function is called to write the result to the CSV log file:

```
csv_report.write_csv_log(HOST, "Python", python_version)
```

167

The `if` block ends by printing the result to the screen:

```
print "Python version = ", python_version
```

Then the function implements an `if` block to determine whether **perl** was entered on the command line. If it was, then the `check_perl()` function is called and the result is assigned to the variable `perl_version`:

```
perl_version = check_versions.check_perl(HOST, USER, PASSWORD)
```

Then the `write_csv_log()` function is called to write the result to the CSV log file:

```
csv_report.write_csv_log(HOST, "Perl", perl_version)
```

The `if` block ends by printing the result to the screen:

```
print "Perl version = ", perl_version
```

check_versions.py

The `check_versions.py` module is responsible for logging into the remote computer, checking the version of the application, and returning the result to the calling program:

```python
import sys
import telnetlib



def check_java(host, user, password):
    java_version = ""
    tn = telnetlib.Telnet(host)
    tn.read_until("login: ")
    tn.write(user + "\n")

    if password:
        tn.read_until("Password: ")
        tn.write(password + "\n")

    tn.write("java -version\n")
    tn.write("exit\n")
    result = tn.read_all()
    result_list = result.split("\n")

    for line in result_list:
```

```python
        if line.startswith("java version"):
            java_version = line[14:21]

    return java_version


def check_python(host, user, password):
    python_version = ""
    tn = telnetlib.Telnet(host)

    tn.read_until("login: ")
    tn.write(user + "\n")
    if password:
        tn.read_until("Password: ")
        tn.write(password + "\n")

    tn.write("python -V\n")
    tn.write("exit\n")
    result = tn.read_all()
    result_list = result.split("\n")

    for line in result_list:
        if line.startswith("Python "):
            python_version = line[7:]

    return python_version


def check_perl(host, user, password):
    perl_version = ""
    tn = telnetlib.Telnet(host)
    tn.read_until("login: ")
    tn.write(user + "\n")
    if password:
        tn.read_until("Password: ")
        tn.write(password + "\n")

    tn.write("perl -version\n")
    tn.write("exit\n")

    result = tn.read_all()
    result_list = result.split("\n")
    for line in result_list:
        if line.startswith("This is perl"):
            perl_version = line[15:20]
    return perl_version
```

check_java()

The check_java() function logs into the identified server and runs the java -version command, which returns the version of Java. It captures the result of that command and returns it to the calling program:

```python
def check_java(host, user, password):
    java_version = ""
    tn = telnetlib.Telnet(host)
    tn.read_until("login: ")
    tn.write(user + "\n")

    if password:
        tn.read_until("Password: ")
        tn.write(password + "\n")

    tn.write("java -version\n")
    tn.write("exit\n")
    result = tn.read_all()
    result_list = result.split("\n")

    for line in result_list:
        if line.startswith("java version"):
            java_version = line[14:21]

    return java_version
```

Why [14:21]?

If you are wondering why I specifically chose the numbers that appear in the preceding example, it's because, for the systems I was looking at, those happened to be the characters that reported the version number. You can play with these values to get the version numbers you want for whatever application you are checking.

After initializing variables, the function opens a Telnet connection to the host:

```python
tn = telnetlib.Telnet(host)
```

The function then logs in, providing username and password:

```python
tn.read_until("login: ")
tn.write(user + "\n")

if password:
    tn.read_until("Password: ")
    tn.write(password + "\n")
```

Then the Java version is captured and the screen output assigned to a variable:

```
tn.write("java -version\n")
tn.write("exit\n")
result = tn.read_all()
```

The Java version is then parsed out of the output of the Telnet session:

```
result_list = result.split("\n")
for line in result_list:
    if line.startswith("java version"):
        java_version = line[14:21]
```

Finally, the Java version is returned to the calling program:

```
return java_version
```

check_python()

The check_python() function logs into the identified server and runs the python -V command, which returns the version of Python. It captures the result of that command and returns it to the calling program:

```
def check_python(host, user, password):
    python_version = ""
    tn = telnetlib.Telnet(host)

    tn.read_until("login: ")
    tn.write(user + "\n")
    if password:
        tn.read_until("Password: ")
        tn.write(password + "\n")

    tn.write("python -V\n")
    tn.write("exit\n")
    result = tn.read_all()
    result_list = result.split("\n")

    for line in result_list:
        if line.startswith("Python "):
            python_version = line[7:]

    return python_version
```

After initializing variables, the function opens a Telnet connection to the host:

```
tn = telnetlib.Telnet(host)
```

The function then logs in, providing username and password:

```
tn.read_until("login: ")
tn.write(user + "\n")

if password:
    tn.read_until("Password: ")
    tn.write(password + "\n")
```

Then the Python version is captured and the screen output assigned to a variable:

```
tn.write("python -V\n")
tn.write("exit\n")
result = tn.read_all()
```

The Python version is then parsed out of the output of the Telnet session:

```
result_list = result.split("\n")
for line in result_list:
    if line.startswith("Python "):
        python_version = line[7:]
```

Finally, the Python version is returned to the calling program:

```
return python_version
```

check_perl()

The check_perl() function logs into the identified server and runs the perl -version command, which queries the version of Perl. It captures the result of that query and returns it to the calling program:

```
def check_perl(host, user, password):
    perl_version = ""
    tn = telnetlib.Telnet(host)
    tn.read_until("login: ")
    tn.write(user + "\n")
    if password:
        tn.read_until("Password: ")
        tn.write(password + "\n")

    tn.write("perl -version\n")
    tn.write("exit\n")

    result = tn.read_all()
    result_list = result.split("\n")
```

```
        for line in result_list:
            if line.startswith("This is perl"):
                perl_version = line[15:20]
        return perl_version
```

After initializing variables, the function opens a Telnet connection to the host:

```
    tn = telnetlib.Telnet(host)
```

The function then logs in, providing username and password:

```
    tn.read_until("login: ")
    tn.write(user + "\n")

    if password:
        tn.read_until("Password: ")
        tn.write(password + "\n")
```

Then the Java version is captured and the screen output assigned to a variable:

```
    tn.write("perl -version\n")
    tn.write("exit\n")
    result = tn.read_all()
```

The Java version is then parsed out of the output of the Telnet session:

```
    tn.write("java -version\n")
    tn.write("exit\n")
    result = tn.read_all()
    result_list = result.split("\n")
for line in result_list:
        if line.startswith("This is perl"):
            perl_version = line[15:20]
```

Finally, the Perl version is returned to the calling program:

```
    return perl_version
```

csv_report.py

The csv_report.py module captures version check information and writes it to the CSV log file.

write_csv_log()

The `write_csv_log()` function writes the version check information to the CSV log file. The log file, `versionchecklog.csv`, is in the program directory. It can be viewed, sorted, and queried with a spreadsheet program.

Here is the function:

```
def write_csv_log(host, application, version):
    today = datetime.datetime.now().strftime("%m/%d/%Y")
    row = [today, host, application, version]
    try:
        writer = csv.writer(open("versionchecklog.csv", "a"))
        writer.writerow(row)
    except:
        print "Error writing to file!"
        sys.exit(1)
```

The first line of the function formats the current date and assigns it to a variable:

```
today = datetime.datetime.now().strftime("%m/%d/%Y")
```

Then it assigns to a list the date, the IP address, the application, and the version:

```
row = [today, host, application, version]
```

Finally, the function uses a `try`/`except` block to open the CSV file and write the row to the CSV file:

```
    try:
        writer = csv.writer(open("versionchecklog.csv", "a"))
        writer.writerow(row)
    except:
        print "Error writing to file!"
        sys.exit(1)
```

Testing

This program takes a multitude of parameters, so that is where testing should be focused. Here are some testing ideas:

❑   Enter all possible combinations of applications, including changing case and changing the order of applications.

❑   Set up a batch file to run a series of IP addresses, to ensure that the system does not time out.

❑   Log in to multiple operating systems, to ensure that there are no issues with that.

Modifying the Program

There are several ways this project could be enhanced, including the following:

❑ Modify the program to accept application names in any format (i.e., uppercase or lowercase).

❑ Modify the program to accept hostnames in addition to IP addresses.

Security Considerations

This program did not take into account two security considerations that would need to be addressed in a real-world scenario:

❑ The program uses a single login and password for every hostname. You could allow command-line arguments to enable users to pass a username and password when the script is run.

❑ Telnet, a protocol that was invented in 1969, is fairly insecure. For increased security, use SSH. (There are open-source Python SSH modules available on the web — just do a Google search and you'll have more tools than you know what to do with.)

Summary

In this chapter, you learned how to use Python as a telnet client, and to capture and process telnet output.

One of the most important domains for an interpreted language like Python is in the area of system administration. Whether it is moving files, checking the status of processes, or (in the case of this project) checking version levels on a list of computers on a network, Python is ideally suited to the task. Being a cross-platform language, it enables you to access Windows, Linux/Unix, and even Macintosh computers if necessary.

8

Content Management System

So far, we've created applications to do many different things — log in to servers, connect to databases, manipulate XML, and the like. However, every program has been created from scratch. What if you don't want to start from scratch? That is what frameworks were built for.

The application in this chapter uses Plone, an open-source Python-based content management system.

What Is a Content Management System?

A *content management system (CMS)* is a system used to manage content. Content management systems are deployed to enable multiple users to create and edit content for access by others, usually on a website — for example, the website Wikipedia.

Plone Overview

Plone is such a large, full-featured application that it makes sense to provide a "10,000 foot" overview of it before diving in to create custom applications.

What Is Plone?

Plone is a content management system with all of the following features:

- ❑   It is multiplatform, meaning it can be run on different operating systems/architectures.
- ❑   It is based on Python.

❑   It is built on Zope, a Python-based application server framework.

❑   It has a scalable interface — nontechnical users can simply enter or edit content, and more knowledgeable users can create custom applications in Python.

❑   It was designed to allow for multiple users and various permission levels.

❑   It is free and extensible.

What You'll Need

In this example, we are installing Plone on Linux. However, you can easily adapt these instructions to install Plone on a Windows or Macintosh system.

This version of Plone installs its own Python distribution — it's great to check Plone out, but it may not be the best solution for a production deployment. Check out the Plone website at `www.plone.org` for more information on Plone distributions.

Installing and Configuring Plone

Installing and configuring Plone involves several steps:

1.   Downloading the current build of Plone for your particular operating system

2.   Extracting the download to an install directory

3.   Running the install

4.   Discovering the admin password

5.   Starting the Plone server

6.   Logging in as admin

7.   Setting up a user

8.   Logging in as the set-up user

These instructions are based on the 3.05 version of Plone, which was current at the time this was written. Subsequent versions may look a little different, but should follow basically the same process.

Downloading Plone

You can get Plone by going to the Plone website at www.plone.org.

The Plone Website

The Plone website (www.plone.org) is itself a great example of the Plone interface. In addition, it offers numerous documents, training videos, links to great books (including a free online one), example applications, and more. It's a place you'll want to spend some time if you implement Plone.

To download Plone:

1. In a web browser, go to www.plone.org. Figure 8-1 shows the Plone home page.

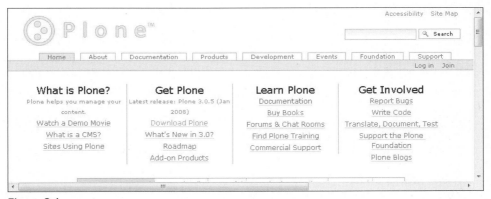

Figure 8-1

2. Click the Download Plone link under the Get Plone heading. You'll then be presented with the screen shown in Figure 8-2, which provides release information.

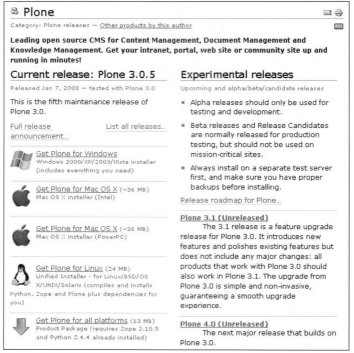

Figure 8-2

3. For this example, Plone is going to be installed on Linux, so click the Get Plone for Linux link. You'll be prompted to download the file. Download it to a temporary location (you could even just put it in a folder on your desktop).

Extracting the Plone Install

After you download the install, you will have a file on your system (wherever you downloaded it) called something like `Plone-3.0.5-UnifiedInstaller.tar.gz`. In a terminal window, in the directory where the file is located, type the following and press Enter:

```
tar -zxvf Plone-3.0.5-UnifiedInstaller.tar
```

This will extract the installation directory. You will now have a directory on your system at the location you chose called `Plone-3.0.5-UnifiedInstaller` (the directory name may be slightly different).

The directory contents will look something like what is shown in Figure 8-3.

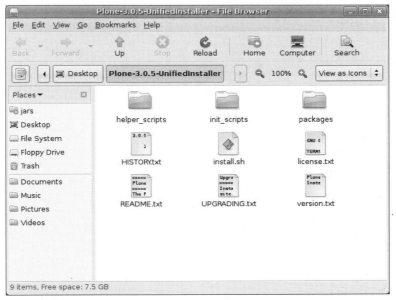

Figure 8-3

Running the Plone Install

Once you have extracted the installation directory, you'll want to run the install. Plone can be installed as the root user or as a non-root user.

Installing as Root User versus Installing as Non-Root User

The non-root method produces an install that will run the Zope server with the same privileges as the installing user. This is probably *not* an acceptable security profile for a production server, but it may be acceptable for testing and development purposes.

The root method produces an install that runs the Zope server as a distinct user identity with minimal privileges (unless you add them). Providing adequate security for a production server requires many more steps, but this is a better starting point.

For the purposes of this example, we'll install as a non-root user.

Logged in as the same user who downloaded and extracted the install, from the Plone-3.0.5-UnifiedInstaller directory, type the following:

```
./install.sh standalone
```

This will install Plone with a single standalone instance of the Zope application server (the simplest installation).

Starting Plone

To start Plone, simply type the following on the command line and press Enter:

```
$HOME/Plone-3.0.5/zinstance/bin/zopectl start
```

Plone is now started and can be connected to.

Discovering the Admin User Password

When Plone is installed, it generates a password for the admin account. To get the password, go to the `$HOME/Plone-3.0.5/zinstance` directory, which should contain a file called `adminPassword.txt`. If you open the file, it will look like the following (in this case, the user who installed Plone was "jars"):

```
Use the account information below to log into the Zope Management Interface
The account has full 'Manager' privileges.

  Username: admin
  Password: sQuv!WX!

Before you start Plone, you should review the settings in:

  /home/jars/Plone-3.0.5/zinstance/etc/zope.conf

Adjust the ports Plone uses before starting the site, if necessary

To start Plone, issue the following command in a Terminal window:

  /home/jars/Plone-3.0.5/zinstance/bin/zopectl start

To stop Plone, issue the following command in a Terminal window:

  /home/jars/Plone-3.0.5/zinstance/bin/zopectl stop
```

As shown in the preceding code, the admin password is located in the file, as well as instructions for how to run Plone.

Logging In as the Admin User

To log in, from a browser go to `http://localhost:8080/Plone` (from the machine on which you installed Plone). You'll see a Login screen like the one shown in Figure 8-4.

Figure 8-4

Enter **admin** in the Login Name text box, and then enter the password found in the `adminPassword`
`.txt` file. You'll then see the Welcome screen shown in Figure 8-5.

Figure 8-5

Setting Up the E-mail Server

You will need to set up an e-mail server to support the e-mailing of passwords to new users.

Log in as the admin user and click the Site Setup link in the upper-right corner. You'll then be presented with the Configuration screen shown in Figure 8-6.

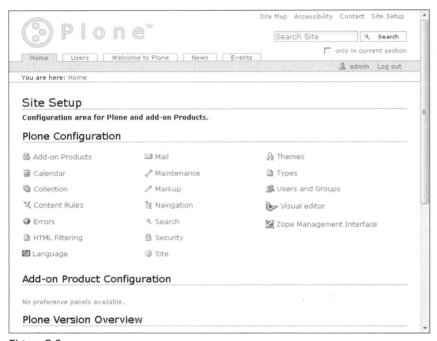

Figure 8-6

At this point, you may get a warning that the mail server hasn't been set up yet. You can continue the install and set up the mail server later.

Click the Mail link. You'll then see the Mail Settings screen shown in Figure 8-7.

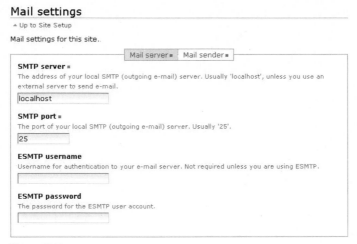

Figure 8-7

Enter the SMTP server IP (assuming the SMTP server is on the same machine where Plone was installed, choose localhost). Click the Save button.

Setting Up a User

One of the first things you'll want to do once you are installed is to set up users. For this example, you'll set up a user named John Smith. Log in as the admin user and click the Site Setup link in the upper-right corner.

Click the Users and Groups link. You'll be presented with the Users Overview screen shown in Figure 8-8.

Figure 8-8

Click the Add New User button. The Personal Details screen shown in Figure 8-9 will appear.

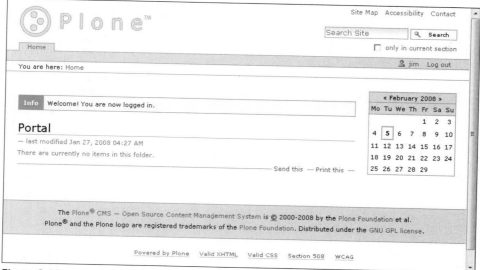

Personal Details

Full Name
Enter full name, eg. John Smith.

User Name ▪
Enter a user name, usually something like 'jsmith'. No spaces or special characters. Usernames and passwords are case sensitive, make sure the caps lock key is not enabled. This is the name used to log in.

E-mail ▪
Enter an email address. This is necessary in case the password is lost. We respect your privacy, and will not give the address away to any third parties or expose it anywhere.

A URL will be generated and e-mailed to you; follow the link to reach a page where you can change your password and complete the registration process.

▸ Register

Figure 8-9

Enter the fields for Full Name, User Name, and E-mail, and then click the Register button.

Logging In as the Set-Up User

You will receive an e-mail message containing the password at the e-mail address you used when you set up the user account. After you have received the e-mailed password, you can log in as that user. Point your browser to http://localhost:8080/Plone (assuming you are running on the computer where you installed Plone). When you log in, you'll see the screen shown in Figure 8-10.

Figure 8-10

Design

Plone has a basic, standard layout, as shown in Figure 8-11 (taken from the plone.org website):

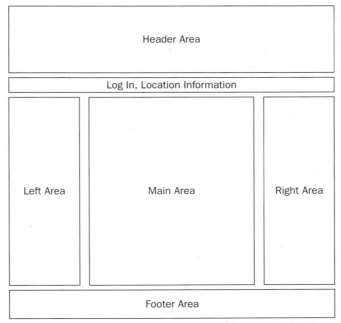

Figure 8-11

Certainly you can deviate from this basic design, but your design should still contain certain elements commonly found on all Plone sites (such as the Login link and the Site Setup link).

As mentioned earlier, the www.plone.org website itself is a great example of a Plone website. Two others include the following, as shown in Figure 8-12 and Figure 8-13, respectively.

- ❏   Discover Magazine: www.discovermagazine.com
- ❏   Free Software Foundation: www.fsf.org

Figure 8-12

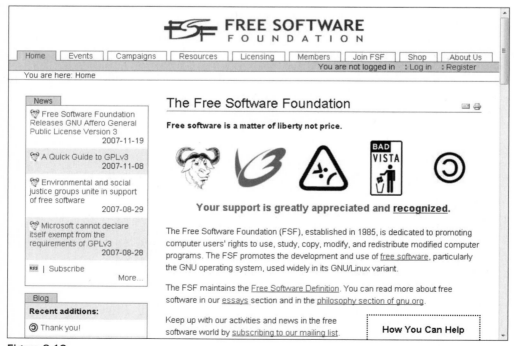

Figure 8-13

Navigation

Generally, a Plone site will contain several common elements:

- ❑ The header area, which is simply the title of the website, usually in large print — optionally with a graphic
- ❑ Login or location information, just below the header area
- ❑ The left area, usually used for navigation
- ❑ The main area, for the main content of your page
- ❑ The right area, for supplemental information (or sometimes advertising)
- ❑ The footer

For a view of how all these elements are arranged, refer to Figure 8-11.

Content Management

The main advantage of content management systems is that they enable you to create content easily. You can create news items and calendar events, post images, and publish many other types of items. For example, from any menu, you can choose the Add New pull-down menu and you'll have several options. We'll go through the process of creating a few common items here.

Creating a Page

Choose the Add New pull-down menu. As shown in Figure 8-14, you are provided with several options.

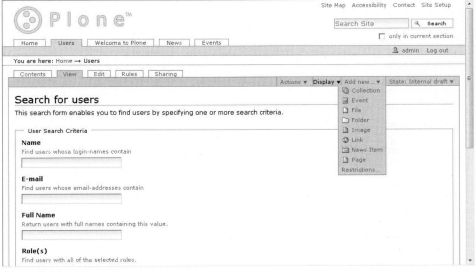

Figure 8-14

Choose a page. You'll be presented with a window in which you can enter page information. The first field is for a title, as shown in Figure 8-15.

Figure 8-15

Enter a title for the page.

The next field is the Description field, as shown in Figure 8-16.

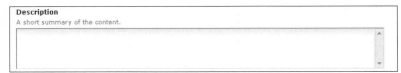

Figure 8-16

Next is the Body Text area, as shown in Figure 8-17.

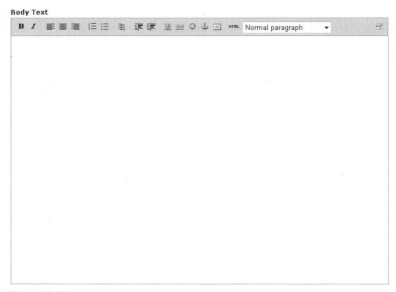

Figure 8-17

As you can see, several rich-text tools are available, enabling you to easily create context for the page. Enter body text information.

At the bottom is a Change note field where you can enter any optional notes relating to the edit you are making on this page, as shown in Figure 8-18.

Figure 8-18

When you are done entering text in all the fields, click the Save button.

Your page will then be displayed, as shown in the example in Figure 8-19.

Figure 8-19

Creating a Collection

A collection is a stored search that can later be accessed anytime you like.

From the Add New pull-down menu, choose Collection. The Add Collection dialog shown in Figure 8-20 will be displayed.

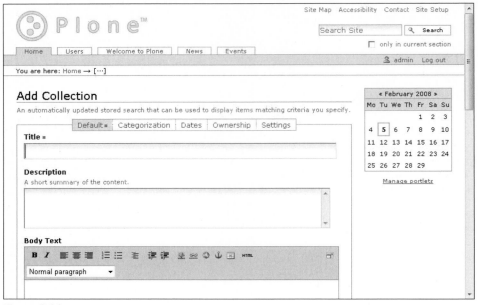

Figure 8-20

Notice that many of the fields are the same as those that appear in the Add a Page dialog. Enter a title, a description, and body text as before. Below those fields are some options unique to the Collection type.

The first set of fields is related to limiting search results, as shown in Figure 8-21.

☐ **Limit Search Results**
If selected, only the 'Number of Items' indicated below will be displayed.

Number of Items
0

Figure 8-21

Entering a value here enables you to limit the number of search results returned to the user, which makes searching faster. For example, if a search that would normally return 500 items is limited to returning 50 items, the search will return much more quickly.

For this example, check the Limit Search Results checkbox and enter **5** for the number of items.

The last set of controls on the page is related to displaying search results as a table, as shown in Figure 8-22.

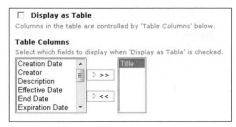

Figure 8-22

This option enables you to show the search results as a table. In addition, you can pick which columns to show in the results table (by default, only the Title column is shown). For this example, check the checkbox and choose all the fields for displaying.

At this point, the bottom part of the page should look like Figure 8-23.

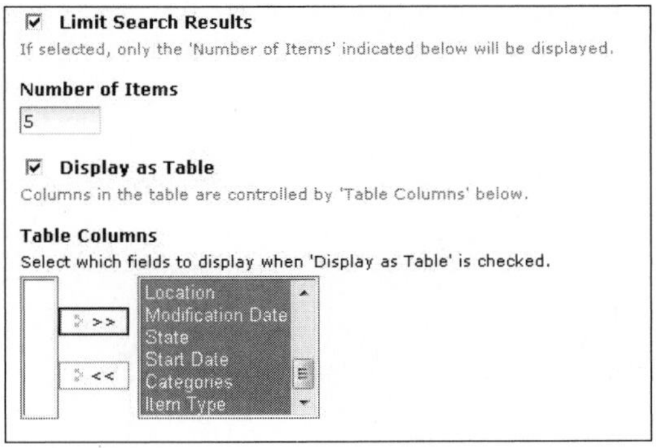

Figure 8-23

Click the Save button. You'll then see the My search collection screen shown in Figure 8-24.

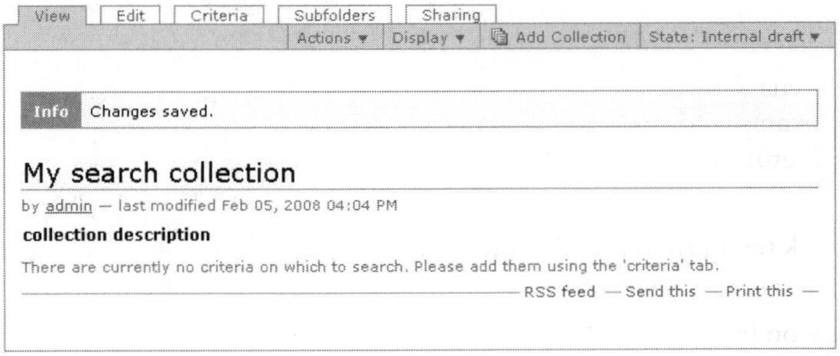

Figure 8-24

As the message on the page indicates, criteria still need to be set up in order for the collection to be functional — in other words, it needs something to search on. Click the Criteria tab to bring up the Criteria dialog shown in Figure 8-25.

Criteria for My search collection

No criteria defined yet. The search will not show any results. Please add criteria below.

┌─ Add New Search Criteria ─────────────────────────┐

Field name
List Available Fields

[Categories ▾]

Criteria type
Criteria does match

[Select values from list ▾]

[⟳ Add criteria]

└───┘

Figure 8-25

There are other options in this dialog, but for this example we will set up date range criteria. Click the Field name drop-down list box and select Creation Date. Then, from the Criteria type drop-down list box, choose Date Range. Click the Add Criteria button. The screen shown in Figure 8-26 will appear.

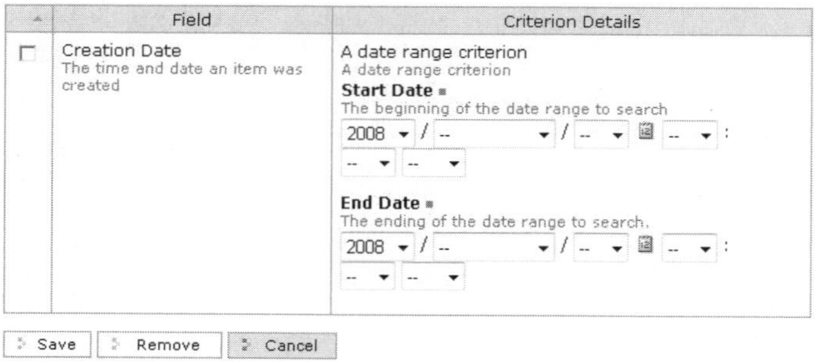

▲	Field	Criterion Details
☐	**Creation Date** The time and date an item was created	A date range criterion A date range criterion **Start Date ▪** The beginning of the date range to search [2008 ▾] / [-- ▾] / [-- ▾] 🖩 [-- ▾] : [-- ▾] [-- ▾] **End Date ▪** The ending of the date range to search. [2008 ▾] / [-- ▾] / [-- ▾] 🖩 [-- ▾] : [-- ▾] [-- ▾]

[⟳ Save] [⟳ Remove] [⟳ Cancel]

Figure 8-26

This screen enables the user to select a data range as the criteria for the search. Enter a range from Jan 1, 2001 to the current day (just to make sure you get some results). Check off "Creation Date" on the left, and then click the Save button. After it saves, click the View tab to look at the results (the content will be different from the example in Figure 8-27, but the display should look the same).

Figure 8-27

Notice that the table runs off the page to the right. The collection can easily be edited to limit the number of fields displayed by clicking the Edit tab and changing the values.

There are many more options available for creating content; covering all of them is beyond the scope of this book. For more Plone resources, please see Appendix B.

User Permissions

Users can be set up with one of several available roles:

- ❑ Contributor
- ❑ Editor
- ❑ Member
- ❑ Reader
- ❑ Reviewer
- ❑ Manager

Each of these roles allows for different permissions in the Plone system. They are based on permissions managed in the underlying Zope framework. For more information, please see the Plone documentation at www.plone.org/documentation.

Summary

This chapter has barely scratched the surface of all the features available in Plone. The great thing about Plone is that it is written in Python, so it can be extended using Python. There are also other frameworks in areas such as the following:

❑ Web frameworks, such as Django and TurboGears

❑ Desktop GUIs, such as GTK and Tk

❑ And many other applications

Part II
Advanced Topics

9

Interacting with the Operating System

Whether a program helps a user balance a checkbook, play a game, write a letter, or connect to a website, all applications share one common feature — they all reside on top of an operating system. Be it Linux, Windows, or some other operating system, most applications (including Python scripts) must interface with the computer through its operating system. As with most scripting languages such as Perl or Ruby, Python has a vast collection of modules to enable the script programmer to interface with the operating system programmatically.

This chapter examines ways to communicate with the operating system through Python. Rather than a single, large application illustrating programming techniques, we will cover many topics with various snippets of code.

The commands and modules covered in this chapter are a small subset of what is available. For complete coverage of operating system services, see the Python Reference Manual.

The chapter covers three main topic areas:

- ❏ **Generic operating system services** — Many features of an operating system are shared among the systems. For example, all operating systems have some way of listing files. Python's ability to access these generic operating system services makes programs more cross-platform.

- ❏ **Windows services** — Python has many features to enable developers to access Windows services, such as the Windows Registry, the Windows Event Viewer, Windows services, and more. Techniques for accessing these services are explored in depth.

- ❏ **Unix/Linux services** — As with Windows, with Unix or Linux there are services specific to the operating systems, such as `syslog` access, password and shadow password services, and others.

Generic Operating System Services

The modules covered in this section are related to operating system services that can be used regardless of the operating system in which the script runs.

The os Module — Generic OS Services

The os module has a unique purpose. It verifies the operating system that the user is running under and then calls the OS-specific function. For example, consider a function written as follows:

```
os.stat
```

If the user is running on Unix or Linux, the stat function in the posix.stat function will be called; whereas if the user is running on Windows, then the nt.stat function will be called. This enables a program to be platform-independent.

Examples

The following sections provide some examples that demonstrate several of the features of the os module.

Example 1

In this first example, a function takes a directory as a parameter, changes to that directory, and outputs the name of the directory and its contents:

```python
import os

def get_directory_info(dir):
    os.chdir(dir)
    current_dir = os.getcwd()
    dir_contents = os.listdir(dir)
    print ""
    print "Current directory = ", current_dir
    print "Directory contents = ", dir_contents
    print""

get_directory_info('C:\\python25')
get_directory_info('C:\\')
```

The output is as follows:

```
Current directory =  C:\python25
Directory contents = ['DLLs', 'Doc', 'include', 'Lib', 'libs', 'python.exe',
'python25.exe', 'pythonw.exe', 'pythonw25.exe', 'tcl', 'Tools', 'w9xpopen.exe']


Current directory =  C:\
Directory contents =  ['$Recycle.Bin', 'autoexec.bat', 'Boot', 'bootmgr',
'BOOTSECT.BAK', 'config.sys', 'Documents and Settings', 'EasyEclipse-for-Python-
1.2.2.2', 'hiberfil.sys', 'jim', 'MSOCache', 'pagefile.sys', 'Program Files',
'ProgramData', 'Python25', 'ruby', 'sqmdata00.sqm', 'sqmnoopt00.sqm', 'System
Volume Information', 'Users', 'Windows']
```

Example 2

This example uses the os.urandom() function. This function randomly generates byte data of a length indicated as a parameter to the function. On a Unix or Linux system, this will query /dev/urandom, and on Windows it will use CryptGenRandom. It can work well for cryptography or passing a unique signature from one program to another:

```python
import os

x = os.urandom(25)
y = x
z = os.urandom(25)

print "Does x = y? ", x==y
print "Does x == z? ", x==z
print "x = ", x
```

The output is as follows:

```
Does x = y?  True
Does x == z?  False
x = 12
```

The time Module — Format and Manipulate System Time

The time module provides various functions related to manipulating and formatting time. The module is always available, but not all functions are available on all platforms. Implementation of some of the functions varies by operating system, so it might be helpful to consult the documentation for your particular OS.

The `time` value is a sequence of nine integers. The return values of `gmtime()`, `localtime()`, and `strptime()` also offer attribute names for individual fields. The following table indicates those attribute names and values:

Index	Attribute	Values
0	tm_year	Example, 2001
1	tm_mon	Range[1-12]
2	tm_mday	Range[1-31]
3	tm_hour	Range[0-23]
4	tm_min	Range[0-59]
5	tm_sec	Range[0-61]
6	tm_wday	Range[0-6]; Monday is 0
7	tm_yday	Range[1-366]
8	tm_isdst	0, 1, -1

Examples

The following examples show the `time` module in action.

Example 1

This example shows the `time()` method, which is a floating-point number expressed in seconds since the epoch (January 1, 1970), in UTC:

```
import time

raw_input("Press the [Enter] key: ")
time1 = time.time()
raw_input("Wait a few seconds, then press the [Enter] key again: ")
time2 = time.time()
difference = int(time2 - time1)

print "There were ",  difference, "seconds bettween the two choices"
```

The output is as follows:

```
Press the [Enter] key:
Wait a few seconds, then press the [Enter] key again:
There were  5 seconds bettween the two choices
```

Example 2

This second example shows some implementations of displaying the time. Time can be shown as a tuple or as a string, and can be formatted in many different ways. In addition, different time representations are provided for (such as local time or Greenwich Mean Time [GMT] offset time):

```
import time

print "GMT Time as tuple: ", time.gmtime()
print "GMT Time as string: ", time.asctime(time.gmtime())
print "Local Time as tuple: ", time.localtime()
print "Local time as string: ", time.asctime(time.localtime())
print "Formatted local time in <month day, year> format: ", \
      time.strftime("%B %d, %Y")
```

The output is as follows:

```
GMT Time as tuple:    (2008, 2, 11, 1, 10, 36, 0, 42, 0)
GMT Time as string:  Mon Feb 11 01:10:36 2008
Local Time as tuple:   (2008, 2, 10, 17, 10, 36, 6, 41, 0)
Local time as string:   Sun Feb 10 17:10:36 2008
Formatted local time in <month day, year> format:   February 10, 2008
```

The optparse Module — Parse Command-Line Options

The optparse module gives you convenient functions for managing command-line options. It has a built-in feature to display help if a user types a --h or --help option.

Example

The following example shows how the optparse module can create options for the user:

```
from optparse import OptionParser

parser = OptionParser()
parser.add_option("-n", "--name", dest="name",
                  help="print name")

(options, args) = parser.parse_args()

print "your name is ", options.name
```

If the user runs the program with the preceding command-line option, the following output results:

```
I:\Applied_Python\Chapter_9>python optparse-example1.py --name "Jim Knowlton"
your name is  Jim Knowlton
```

If the program is run with a `--h` option, then this is the output:

```
I:\Applied_Python\Chapter_9>python optparse-example1.py --h
Usage: optparse-example1.py [options]

Options:
  -h, --help             show this help message and exit
  -n NAME, --name=NAME   print name
```

The platform Module — Get Platform Information

The `platform` module includes both platform-specific functions and cross-platform functions. This section addresses the cross-platform capability. The `platform` module enables you to query for both hardware and software platform information. You can then parse the information returned and act accordingly in your script.

Example

The following example demonstrates how to query for a particular operating system and then branch the code based on the operating system in which the script is running:

```
import platform

if platform.system() == 'Windows':
    print "The platform is Windows"
    #put Windows-specific code here
elif platform.system() == 'Linux':
    print "The platform is Linux"
    #put Linux-specific code here
```

If the script is run on a Windows box, then it will return the following message:

```
The platform is Windows
```

If the script is run on a Linux box, then it will return this message:

```
The platform is Linux
```

The getpass Module — Generate and Check Passwords

The `getpass` module provides functionality to prompt the user for a password, and enables a script to authenticate the user based on whether the correct password was entered. It also has a function to return the login of the currently logged-in user.

Example

The following example prompts for a password and if the correct password is entered, displays the login of the currently logged-in user:

```
import getpass

password = getpass.getpass()

if password == "letmein":
    print("Logged in username is " + getpass.getuser())
```

Some Other Things You Can Do

This, of course, is just a sampling of the cross-platform operating system functionality available through Python. Here are a few other areas to look into:

❑   The `curses` module provides access to the curses library, for portable advanced terminal handling.

❑   The `logging` module assists in managing generic system logs.

❑   The `errno` module enables a script to translate error codes to error descriptions.

Accessing Windows Services

The following modules reflect some popular ways to access Windows services through Python.

You'll notice there isn't any coverage of Windows UI programming here. Although it certainly can be done, such a discussion is beyond the scope of this book.

The winreg Module — Manipulate the Windows Registry

The Windows Registry is a database that contains program and system information and settings. Often it can be useful to access the Registry (to read from it or write to it) via a script. The `winreg` module makes this easy to do in Python.

Example

The following example queries a particular key in the Registry and outputs all the subkeys for that key:

```
import _winreg

explorer = _winreg.OpenKey(
    _winreg.HKEY_CURRENT_USER,
    "Software\\Microsoft\\Windows\\CurrentVersion\\Explorer")

# list values owned by this registry key
i = 0
try:
    while 1:
        name, value, type = _winreg.EnumValue(explorer, i)
        print repr(name),
        i += 1
except:
    print
```

The following is the output for this program:

```
I:\Applied_Python\Chapter_9>python winreg-example1.py
'ShellState' 'CleanShutdown' 'Browse For Folder Width' 'Browse For Folder Height
' 'link' 'Logon User Name'
```

The winsound Module

The winsound module enables a script to access the sound-playing functionality of Windows platforms. It includes functions and several built-in constants. The module enables a script to play Windows system sounds or WAV files.

Example

The following example shows how to play various sounds with the winsound module:

```
import winsound

print "Play Windows exit sound."
winsound.PlaySound("SystemExit", winsound.SND_ALIAS)

print "Probably play Windows default sound"
winsound.PlaySound("*", winsound.SND_ALIAS)

print "Play a message beep"
winsound.MessageBeep()

print "Play an evil laugh"
winsound.PlaySound('evil_laugh.wav',winsound.SND_FILENAME)
```

As shown in the preceding example, the `PlaySound()` function has two parameters. The first parameter contains either audio data formatted as a string, a WAV file, or nothing. Its second parameter is a constant that tells the function what to do. The following table describes the available constants.

Constant Name	Description
SND_LOOP	Play the sound repeatedly. The `SND_ASYNC` flag must also be used to avoid blocking. Cannot be used with `SND_MEMORY`.
SND_MEMORY	The sound parameter to `PlaySound()` is a memory image of a WAV file, as a string.
SND_PURGE	Stop playing all instances of the specified sound.
SND_ASYNC	Returns immediately, allowing sounds to play asynchronously.
SND_NODEFAULT	If the specified sound cannot be found, do not play the system default sound.
SND_NOSTOP	Do not interrupt sounds currently playing.
SND_NOWAIT	Return immediately if the sound driver is busy.
MB_ICONASTERISK	Play the `SystemDefault` sound.
MB_ICONEXCLAMATION	Play the `SystemExclamation` sound.
MB_ICONHAND	Play the `SystemHand` sound.
MB_ICONQUESTION	Play the `SystemQuestion` sound.
MB_OK	Play the `SystemDefault` sound.

The `MessageBeep()` function takes an optional parameter of audio data formatted as a string. If no parameter is given (as in the preceding example), the `MB_OK` sound is played.

The win32serviceutil Module — Manage Windows Services

Windows services are processes that run on a Windows desktop or a Windows server machine. They can be remotely started, stopped, restarted, and queried for status. To manage Windows services, there is the `win32serviceutil` module, found in Mark Hammond's `win32all` package.

For information on how to get the `win32all` package, please see Appendix B.

Example

The following example shows how to start a service, stop a service, restart a service, or get service status through Python:

```python
import win32serviceutil, time

def service_info(action, machine, service):
    if action == 'stop':
        win32serviceutil.StopService(service, machine)
        print '%s stopped successfully' % service
        time.sleep(3)
    elif action == 'start':
        win32serviceutil.StartService(service, machine)
        print '%s started successfully' % service
        time.sleep(3)
    elif action == 'restart':
        win32serviceutil.RestartService(service, machine)
        print '%s restarted successfully' % service
        time.sleep(3)
    elif action == 'status':
        if win32serviceutil.QueryServiceStatus(service, machine)[1] == 4:
            print "%s is running normally" % service
        else:
            print "%s is *not* running" % service

machine = 'localhost'
service = 'RemoteRegistry'

service_info('start', machine, service)
service_info('stop', machine, service)
service_info('start', machine, service)
service_info('restart', machine, service)
service_info('status', machine, service)
```

Because this example is a little longer than the others, let's examine it section by section.

The `service_info` function takes an action, a machine, and a service name as parameters:

```python
def service_info(action, machine, service):
```

The rest of the function is simply an `if` structure that performs actions on the service based on the action parameter passed in:

```
    if action == 'stop':
        win32serviceutil.StopService(service, machine)
        print '%s stopped successfully' % service
        time.sleep(3)
    elif action == 'start':
        win32serviceutil.StartService(service, machine)
        print '%s started successfully' % service
        time.sleep(3)
    elif action == 'restart':
        win32serviceutil.RestartService(service, machine)
        print '%s restarted successfully' % service
        time.sleep(3)
    elif action == 'status':
        if win32serviceutil.QueryServiceStatus(service, machine)[1] == 4:
            print "%s is running normally" % service
        else:
            print "%s is *not* running" % service
```

This function could be accessed by another program by importing the module, but in this case we want to be able to run the program, so some code is added at the bottom of the program to run the function multiple times, with different parameters:

```
machine = 'localhost'
service = 'RemoteRegistry'

service_info('start', machine, service)
service_info('stop', machine, service)
service_info('start', machine, service)
service_info('restart', machine, service)
service_info('status', machine, service)
```

When the program is run, it generates the following output:

```
RemoteRegistry started successfully
RemoteRegistry stopped successfully
RemoteRegistry started successfully
RemoteRegistry restarted successfully
RemoteRegistry is running normally
```

The win32net Module — Access Windows Networking Features

The win32net module, also part of Mark Hammond's win32all library of modules, includes many functions and constants to make the management of Windows networks easier. This module enables you to add, modify, delete, enumerate, and query for users, groups, shares, servers, and networks.

Example

The following example enumerates the users, groups, shares, and servers found on a computer. In this example, it simply searches the local machine, but it could easily be modified to enable selecting and authenticating to a remote computer:

```python
import win32net

#print users
users = win32net.NetUserEnum('localhost', 0)
print "USERS"
print "=========="
for user in users[0]:
    print user['name'] + "\n"

#print groups
groups = win32net.NetGroupEnum('localhost', 0)
print "GROUPS"
print "=========="
for group in groups[0]:
    print group['name'] + "\n"

#print shares
shares = win32net.NetShareEnum('localhost', 0)
print "SHARES"
print "=========="
for share in shares[0]:
    print share['netname'] + "\n"

#print servers
servers = win32net.NetServerEnum(None, 100)
print "SERVERS"
print "=========="
for server in servers[0]:
    print server['name'] + "\n"
```

As you can see, the `win32net` module provides functions that enable you to enumerate different network objects. It also enables you to perform other operations, such as the following:

❑ Adding objects

❑ Deleting objects

❑ Editing object properties

❑ Changing the level of information returned (verbosity)

The results returned depend entirely on the particular information found, but here is the output that resulted from running the script on my system:

```
I:\Applied_Python\Chapter_9>python win32net-example1.py
USERS
==========
Administrator
Guest
jim
jim user
__vmware_user__

GROUPS
==========
None

SHARES
==========
ADMIN$
C$
IPC$
share of jim

SERVERS
==========
JIM-PC
```

Some Other Things You Can Do

In addition to what has been discussed in this section, there are many more ways to integrate a Python script with Windows, including the following:

- ❏   win32crypt to use Windows encryption to copy protect data
- ❏   win32file to interface with Windows' file APIs
- ❏   win32inet to interact with Internet protocols through Windows
- ❏   wincerapi to actually write Python applications to interface with Windows CE

For more information, be sure to check out Appendix A, which will point you toward some great resources for programming with Python in Windows, including a book by Mark Hammond, the creator of the win32api *library for which much of this example code is written.*

Accessing Unix/Linux Services

The following examples demonstrate some ways in which Python scripts can interact with a Linux or Unix system.

These examples were run on a computer running Ubuntu Linux 7.10. However, the examples should run on any version of Unix.

The termios Module — Access Unix-Style TTY Interface

The termios module provides an interface to tty I/O control. For a complete description of these calls, see the Linux or Unix manual pages. It is only available for those Unix versions that support POSIX termios style tty I/O control. All functions in this module take a file descriptor as their first argument. This can be an integer, such as what is contained in sys.stdin.fileno(), or a file object, such as sys.stdin itself.

Example

The following example shows the termios module being used to accept a password without echoing the password to the screen, and returning the password to the caller:

```
def getpass(prompt = "Password: "):
    import termios, sys
    fd = sys.stdin.fileno()
    old = termios.tcgetattr(fd)
    new = termios.tcgetattr(fd)
    new[3] = new[3] & ~termios.ECHO          # lflags
    try:
        termios.tcsetattr(fd, termios.TCSADRAIN, new)
        passwd = raw_input(prompt)
    finally:
        termios.tcsetattr(fd, termios.TCSADRAIN, old)
    return passwd

password = getpass()
if password == "zanzibar":
    print "Let you in"
else:
    print "Access denied"
```

The resource Module — Manage Unix System Resources

The resource module provides a mechanism for managing and controlling the amount of resources used by a particular program. It has several functions available, and makes use of a list of constants related to system resources.

Example

The example makes use of the `getrusage()` function. It returns a tuple that contains 16 different data items related to system resource usage. The following table shows all the data items returned.

Index	Field	Resource
0	ru_utime	Time in user mode (float)
1	ru_stime	Time in system mode (float)
2	ru_maxrss	Maximum resident set size
3	ru_ixrss	Shared memory size
4	ru_idrss	Unshared memory size
5	ru_isrss	Unshared stack size
6	ru_minflt	Page faults not requiring I/O
7	ru_majflt	Page faults requiring I/O
8	ru_nswap	Number of swap-outs
9	ru_inblock	Block input operations
10	ru_oublock	Block output operations
11	ru_msgsnd	Messages sent
12	ru_msgrcv	Messages received
13	ru_nsignals	Signals received
14	ru_nvcsw	Voluntary context switches
15	ru_nivcsw	Involuntary context switches

Here is the entire example:

```
import resource

resourcelist = ['time in user mode',
'time in system mode',
'maximum resident set size',
'shared memory size',
'unshared memory size',
'unshared stack size',
'page faults not requiring I/O',
'page faults requiring I/O',
```

(continued)

(continued)

```
    'number of swap outs',
    'block input operations',
    'block output operations',
    'messages sent',
    'messages received',
    'signals received',
    'voluntary context switches',
    'involuntary context switches']

getresource = resource.getrusage(resource.RUSAGE_SELF)

for i, item in enumerate(resourcelist):
        print item, ": ", getresource[i]
```

Now let's go through the example. First, a list is created with the text for all the items:

```
resourcelist = ['time in user mode',
    'time in system mode',
    'maximum resident set size',
    'shared memory size',
    'unshared memory size',
    'unshared stack size',
    'page faults not requiring I/O',
    'page faults requiring I/O',
    'number of swap outs',
    'block input operations',
    'block output operations',
    'messages sent',
    'messages received',
    'signals received',
    'voluntary context switches',
    'involuntary context switches']
```

Then the `getrusage()` function is run, and its output is assigned to the list `getresource`:

```
getresource = resource.getrusage(resource.RUSAGE_SELF)
```

Finally, a `for` loop is used to output the information to the screen in a readable way:

```
for i, item in enumerate(resourcelist):
        print item, ": ", getresource[i]
```

When the program is run, the output looks like this:

```
time in user mode :    0.016001
time in system mode :    0.008
maximum resident set size :    0
shared memory size :    0
unshared memory size :    0
unshared stack size :    0
page faults not requiring I/O :    733
page faults requiring I/O :    0
number of swap outs :    0
block input operations :    0
block output operations :    0
messages sent :    0
messages received :    0
signals received :    0
voluntary context switches :    1
involuntary context switches :    4
```

The syslog Module — Access the Unix syslog

Python's `syslog` module enables you to access the `syslog`, write log entries, and read the log.

Example

The following example enables users to choose a log priority and enter a message. It then reports the status of the attempt to write to the `syslog`:

```
import syslog

print """
Enter a number and press [Enter]:
1 - Emergency
2 - Alert
3 - Critical
4 - Error
5 - Warning
6 - Notics
7 - Info
8 - Debug
"""
choice = raw_input("")

message = raw_input("Type the log message and press [Enter]: ")

if choice == '1':
        log_priority = syslog.LOG_EMERG
```

(continued)

(continued)

```
elif choice == '2':
        log_priority = syslog.LOG_ALERT
elif choice == '3':
        log_priority = syslog.LOG_CRIT
elif choice == '4':
        log_priority = syslog.LOG_ERR
elif choice == '5':
        log_priority = syslog.LOG_WARNING
elif choice == '6':
        log_priority = syslog.LOG_NOTICE
elif choice == '7':
        log_priority = syslog.LOG_INFO
elif choice == '8':
        log_priority = syslog.LOG_DEBUG

try:
        syslog.syslog(log_priority, message)
        print "log entry recorded"
except:
        print "problem writing to syslog"
        raise
```

The first section of the program simply presents a menu so that the user can choose a log priority:

```
print """
Enter a number and press [Enter]:
1 - Emergency
2 - Alert
3 - Critical
4 - Error
5 - Warning
6 - Notics
7 - Info
8 - Debug
"""
choice = raw_input("")
```

Then the user is prompted for the message to be written to the log:

```
message = raw_input("Type the log message and press [Enter]: ")
```

Based on the user's selection, the program then assigns the log priority:

```
if choice == '1':
        log_priority = syslog.LOG_EMERG
elif choice == '2':
        log_priority = syslog.LOG_ALERT
elif choice == '3':
        log_priority = syslog.LOG_CRIT
elif choice == '4':
        log_priority = syslog.LOG_ERR
elif choice == '5':
        log_priority = syslog.LOG_WARNING
elif choice == '6':
        log_priority = syslog.LOG_NOTICE
elif choice == '7':
        log_priority = syslog.LOG_INFO
elif choice == '8':
        log_priority = syslog.LOG_DEBUG
```

Finally, the `syslog` is written to, and the status is returned:

```
try:
        syslog.syslog(log_priority, message)
        print "log entry recorded"
except:
        print "problem writing to syslog"
        raise
```

The commands Module — Run Commands and Get Output

The `commands` module enables you to run system commands and capture the status of the system and the output generated by the command. It consists of the `getstatus()`, `getoutput()`, and `getstatusoutput()` functions:

- ❑ `getstatus(file)` — Returns the output of `"ls -ld file"` to a string
- ❑ `getoutput(command)` — Returns the output of a command as a string
- ❑ `getstatusoutput(command)` — Returns a tuple containing a status code representing the state of the system, and the output of the command

Example

Following is an example showing each of the functions in action:

```
import commands

print r"output of commands.getstatusoutput('ls /usr/local')"
output1 = commands.getstatusoutput('ls /usr/local')
print output1
print ""

print r"output of commands.getstatusoutput('cat /bin/junk')"
output2 = commands.getstatusoutput('cat /bin/junk')
print output2
print ""

print r"output of commands.getoutput('ls /usr/local')"
output3 = commands.getoutput('ls /usr/local')
print output3
print ""

print r"output of commands.getstatus('/usr/local')"
output4 = commands.getstatus('/usr/local')
print output4
print ""
```

Here is what the screen output looks like for this example:

```
output of commands.getstatusoutput('ls /usr/local')
(0, 'bin\netc\ngames\ninclude\nlib\nman\nsbin\nshare\nsrc')

output of commands.getstatusoutput('cat /bin/junk')
(256, 'cat: /bin/junk: No such file or directory')

output of commands.getoutput('ls /usr/local')
bin
etc
games
include
lib
man
sbin
share
src

output of commands.getstatus('/usr/local')
drwxr-xr-x 10 root root 4096 2007-10-16 01:17 /usr/local
```

Some Other Things You Can Do

There are many, many ways to interact with a Linux/Unix system in Python. Here are some modules to check out:

❑   `posix` enables you to access operating system functionality through the POSIX interface.

❑   `grp` provides access to the group database.

❑   `pwd` provides access to the password database.

❑   `pipes` provides an interface to shell pipelines.

❑   `nis` provides access to Sun's NIS directory (Yellow Pages).

Summary

This chapter has touched on many different techniques for interacting with the operating system. Generic operating system modules are those that can be used regardless of the operating system in which the script is run. This chapter covered the following modules:

❑   The `os` module verifies the operating system that the user is running under, and then calls the OS-specific function.

❑   The `time` module provides various functions related to manipulating and formatting time.

❑   The `optparse` module gives you convenient functions to manage command-line options.

❑   The `platform` module has platform-specific functions and cross-platform functions.

❑   The `getpass` module provides functionality to prompt the user for a password, and enables a script to authenticate the user based on whether or not a correct password was entered.

Windows-based modules enable a script to access Windows features. This chapter covered the following Windows-based modules:

❑   The `winreg` module enables a script to read to and write from the Windows Registry.

❑   The `winsound` module enables a script to access the sound-playing functionality of Windows platforms.

❑   The `win32serviceutil` module, found in Mark Hammond's `win32all` package, enables a Python script to manage Windows services.

❑   The `win32net` module, also part of Mark Hammond's `win32all` library of modules, has many functions and constants to make management of Windows networks easier.

This chapter provided several examples demonstrating how Python scripts can interact with a Linux or Unix system:

❑ The `termios` module provides an interface to `tty` I/O control.

❑ The `resource` module provides a mechanism for managing and controlling the amount of resources used by a particular program.

❑ Python's `syslog` module enables you to access the `syslog` to write log entries and read the log.

❑ The `commands` module enables you to run system commands and capture the status of the system and the output generated by the command.

10

Debugging and Testing

All of the projects from the previous chapters — whether it was a project that accessed files on the file system, interacted with a database, or served pages on a web server — have one thing in common: They didn't work the first time.

It is inevitable as a programmer that you will run into errors in your programs. Fortunately, Python has built-in features to help you discover those "bugs" and take care of them:

❑ The Python debugger (which is actually just another Python module itself) supports setting decision markers called *breakpoints* and allows you to "step" through code one line at a time. It supports very sophisticated debugging if needed, including providing a stack viewer.

❑ There are several Python automated test frameworks that enable you to build automated tests to test your code. Having automated tests enables you to add functionality and run your tests to verify that you haven't broken anything.

The Python Debugger

The basic purpose of a debugger is to enable a developer to "walk" through a program as it executes, noticing specific areas where the program breaks, and where it could be modified or optimized to work better.

Running the Debugger

The Python debugger can be utilized in several different ways:

Importing the pdb Module Directly

The `pdb` module is the Python debugger. You can access it by importing it directly either in a script or in the Python console:

```
Import pdb
```

With the debugger module imported, you then have access to many different functions for debugging. This is especially useful if you import the module from Python's interactive interpreter, so let's look at an example of doing that now.

Download the supplemental code from the website for Chapter 10. From that directory, launch the Python interpreter. You'll see a screen like the following:

```
ActivePython 2.5.1.1 (ActiveState Software Inc.) based on
Python 2.5.1 (r251:54863, May  1 2007, 17:47:05) [MSC v.1310 32 bit (Intel)] on
win32
Type "help", "copyright", "credits" or "license" for more information.
>>>
```

The first thing to do is to import the Python debugger. Type **import pdb** and press Enter. You'll get the >>> Python prompt back.

At this point, import the test module created for this example, called `pdbtest`. Do this by typing **import pdbtest** and pressing Enter. The screen should now look like the following:

```
ActivePython 2.5.1.1 (ActiveState Software Inc.) based on
Python 2.5.1 (r251:54863, May  1 2007, 17:47:05) [MSC v.1310 32 bit (Intel)] on
win32
Type "help", "copyright", "credits" or "license" for more information.
>>> import pdb
>>> import pdbtest
>>>
```

> **What Is pdbtest?**
>
> The `pdbtest` module is simply a test program we are using to demonstrate the `pdb` debugger. Here is the code for it:
>
> ```
> def testfunction():
>     name = raw_input("Enter your name: ")
>     if name == "Jim":
>         print "Hello Jim!"
>     else:
>         print "You're not Jim - good bye."
> ```

Now the Python debugger does its work. Run the Debugger's `run()` method by typing the following and pressing Enter:

```
pdb.run('pdbtest.testfunction()')
```

This will start the debugger and give you the following prompt:

```
> <string>(1)<module>()
(Pdb)
```

At this point, the debugger is waiting for you to tell it what to do. The most common commands are as follows:

❑   **Step** — Tells the debugger to execute only the next line of code, and then stop

❑   **Next** — Continues execution until the next line in the current function is reached; otherwise, it returns

❑   **Return** — Continues execution until the current function returns

❑   **Continue** — Tells the debugger to run the program normally from that point, without pausing

This is just a sampling of the Python debugger commands available—for the complete list of commands, see the official Python documentation at www.python.org.

Accessing the Python Debugger through IDLE

If you are running IDLE, there is a menu for debugging features, as shown in Figure 10-1.

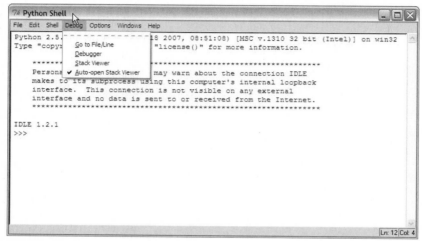

Figure 10-1

As shown in Figure 10-1, there are several options:

❑ **Go to File/Line** — Looks around the insertion point for a filename and line number, opens the file, and shows the line

❑ **Debugger** — Opens a Debugger UI (discussed below) and runs commands in the shell under the debugger

❑ **Stack Viewer** — Shows the stack viewer for the most recent exception/traceback

❑ **Auto-open Stack Viewer** — Opens the stack viewer automatically every time there is an exception/traceback

The Debug menu is only available in IDLE from the Python Shell window, not from a window in which you are editing a Python file.

The Debug Control window

The Debug Control window is shown in Figure 10-2.

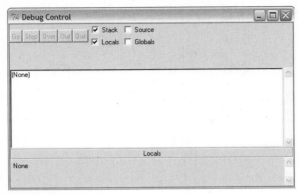

Figure 10-2

As shown in the figure, this window has several main areas:

❑ Five buttons that enable you to interact with the debugger:

    ❑ **Go** — Runs the program without pause

    ❑ **Step** — Executes only the next line

    ❑ **Over** — Skips the next line

    ❑ **Out** — Jumps out of a loop

    ❑ **Quit** — Quits the running program (but keeps the debugger running)

❑ Four checkboxes that enable you to select what to monitor:

    ❑ Stack

    ❑ Source

    ❑ Locals

    ❑ Globals

❑ A message window displaying debugger messages

❑ A Variables area at the bottom (depending on what you chose to monitor)

Example

Let's explore a brief example to show how the debugger works:

1. From the Python Shell in IDLE, select Debug ➪ Debugger.

2. In the debugger, select Stack and Globals, and ensure that Source and Locals are deselected.

3. In the Python Shell, type the following command: **name = "jim"**.

You can use your own name if you like. After doing that, the debugger window should look something like what is shown in Figure 10-3.

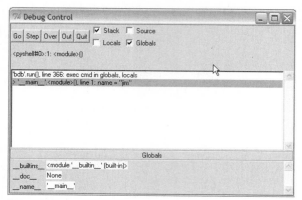

Figure 10-3

Notice that you don't have your prompt back yet in the Python Shell. That's because the command has not actually been executed yet. Click the Step button. The command is executed and the prompt is back in the Python Shell.

Python Test Frameworks

After a program is written, there is a tendency to feel a sense of great accomplishment, to feel like the work is done. This is, however, not true. A program must be tested.

Why We Test

A program is only "done" when it can be verified that it accomplishes two things:

❑ **"It does the thing right"** — The program must be implemented in the way intended by the program design.

❑ **"It does the right thing"** — The program, as implemented, must actually solve the problem it was intended to solve.

This may seem redundant, so perhaps it can be illustrated best with an example. Let's say the goal is to have a program that enables users to log in to a website and view information about their local machine, such as user accounts and groups. However, suppose that in designing the program, the information is sent across the network in plain text. The program was implemented in exactly the way intended, but the problem was the intention itself — sending local account information across the Internet in plain text is a bad idea, as it is extremely insecure.

Therefore, by testing, we are verifying not only the *implementation*, but also the *intention*.

Unit Testing

Unit testing is simply testing a *unit* of code, rather than testing the entire program. The snapshothelper.py module from Chapter 2 is a good example to look at. Since I am going to refer to it several times in this section, let's look at it now:

```python
import os, pickle, difflib, sys, pprint

def createSnapshot(directory, filename):
    cumulative_directories = []
    cumulative_files = []

    for root, dirs, files in os.walk(directory):
        cumulative_directories = cumulative_directories + dirs
        cumulative_files = cumulative_files + files

    try:
        output = open(filename, 'wb')
        pickle.dump(cumulative_directories, output, -1)
        pickle.dump(cumulative_files, output, -1)
        output.close()
    except:
        print "Problems encounted trying to save snapshot file!"

    raw_input("Press [Enter] to continue...")
    return

def listSnapshots(extension):
    snaplist = []
    filelist = os.listdir(os.curdir)
    for item in filelist:
        if item.find(extension) != -1:
            snaplist.append(item)

    print '''
Snapshot list:
=========================
'''
    printList(snaplist)

    raw_input("Press [Enter] to continue...")


def compareSnapshots(snapfile1, snapfile2):

    try:
        pkl_file = open(snapfile1, 'rb')
        dirs1 = pickle.load(pkl_file)
```

(continued)

(continued)

```python
            files1 = pickle.load(pkl_file)
            pkl_file.close()

            pk2_file = open(snapfile2, 'rb')
            dirs2 = pickle.load(pk2_file)
            files2 = pickle.load(pk2_file)
            pk2_file.close()
        except:
            print "Problems encountered accessing snapshot files!"
            raw_input("\n\nPress [Enter] to continue...")
            return

        result_dirs = list(difflib.unified_diff(dirs1, dirs2))
        result_files = list(difflib.unified_diff(files1, files2))

        added_dirs = []
        removed_dirs = []
        added_files = []
        removed_files = []

        for result in result_files:
            if result.find("\n") == -1:
                if result[0] == "+":
                    resultadd = result.strip('+')
                    added_files.append(resultadd)
                elif result[0] == "-":
                    resultsubtract = result.strip('-')
                    removed_files.append(resultsubtract)

        for result in result_dirs:
            if result.find("\n") == -1:
                if result[0] == "+":
                    resultadd = result.strip('+')
                    added_dirs.append(resultadd)
                elif result[0] == "-":
                    resultsubtract = result.strip('-')
                    removed_dirs.append(resultsubtract)

        print "\n\nAdded Directories:\n"
        printList(added_dirs)
        print "\n\nAdded Files:\n"
        printList(added_files)
        print "\n\nRemoved Directories:\n"
        printList(removed_dirs)
        print "\n\nRemoved Files:\n"
        printList(removed_files)
        raw_input("\n\nPress [Enter] to continue...")

def showHelp():
    os.system('cls')
    print '''
DIRECTORY/FILE COMPARISON TOOL
====================================
```

```
        Welcome to the directory/file snapshot tool.  This tool
        allows you to create snapshots of a directory/file tree,
        list the snapshots you have created in the current directory,
        and compare two snapshots, listing any directories and files
        added or deleted between the first snapshot and the second.

        To run the program follow the following procedure:
        1.  Create a snapshot
        2.  List snapshot files
        3.  Compare snapshots
        4.  Help (this screen)
        5.  Exit


        '''
        raw_input("Press [Enter] to continue...")

def invalidChoice():
    print "INVALID CHOICE, TRY AGAIN!"
    raw_input("\n\nPress [Enter] to continue...")
    return


def printList(list):
    fulllist = ""
    indexnum = 1

    if len(list) > 20:
        for item in list:
            print "\t\t" + item,
            if (indexnum)%3 == 0:
                print "\n"
            indexnum = indexnum + 1
    else:
        for item in list:
            print "\t" + item
```

This program could simply be run and verified, but if, for example, you wanted to test just the createSnapshot() function, you would only need to test that portion, or "unit." This is done with a unit test. It involves passing to that unit its needed parameters, and then using some mechanism (such as assertions) to verify that the expected behavior is occurring.

Manual Unit Testing with the Python Interactive Interpreter

A unique feature of Python is its ability to test specific functions using the interactive interpreter. Using the Python interpreter, you can import a module and run a specific function, passing it values and then using the unittest module to assert that particular conditions are true.

> ## Why Testers Should Befriend the Python Interactive Interpreter
>
> The great thing for testers about the Python interactive interpreter is that you can modify your testing on-the-fly as you test. It gives you the framework and libraries of automated testing but with the spontaneity of exploratory testing.

To begin, start the Python interpreter, and then import the `snapshothelper.py` module with the following command (assuming you are running Python from the directory where you downloaded this chapter's files):

```
import snaphothelper
```

Now the function can be run, with parameters you choose. In this case, the `createSnapshot()` function will be run, passing the directory to create a snapshot of, along with the filename to create:

```
snapshothelper.createSnapshot('c:\\python25', 'python25snap.snp')
```

The function is then run with the parameters specified.

To verify that the file was created, you could use a DOS prompt or Unix terminal, but as long as the Python interpreter is up, let's do it through that.

Import the `os` module and then type the following in the interpreter window (yes, there's a typo here — type it exactly as shown):

```
assert 'python25snap.snp1' in os.listdir(os.curdir), "File did not get created"
```

> ## About the assert Statement
>
> The format of the `assert` statement is `assert statement1, statement2`. Basically, it works as follows: If statement 1 is true, then statement 2 is not executed.

Did you get an error? Good! Your screen should look like this:

```
>>> assert 'pythonsnap.snp1' in os.listdir(os.curdir), "File did not get created"
Traceback (most recent call last):
  File "<stdin>", line 1, in <module>
AssertionError: File did not get created
```

As you can see, the assertion returns a traceback, and prints the error message defined in the `assert` statement.

Let's try the statement again, this time using the correct filename:

```
assert 'python25snap.snp' in os.listdir(os.curdir), "File did not get created"
```

Nothing happened? That's exactly right. If an assertion is true, it simply continues, which in this case means returning the interpreter prompt.

unittest — Python's Default Unit Test Framework

Python comes with a unit testing module out of the box, called `unittest`, also referred to as *PyUnit*. It is a Python-language version of the popular JUnit test framework for Java, written by Kent Beck and Erich Gamma.

`unittest` supports the following:

❑   Automation of tests

❑   Setup and shutdown functions, which enable sharing of functionality among all tests

❑   Aggregating tests into suites

❑   Separating tests from the reporting framework

To accomplish these features, `unittest` implements several concepts:

❑   **Test fixture** — This is the "housekeeping" needed to perform associated tests, and any necessary cleanup actions, such as deleting temporary files.

❑   **Test case** — A test case is the smallest unit of testing. At the most basic level, it consists of executing some code and testing the behavior of the code against a predetermined standard.

❑   **Test suite** — A test suite is simply a collection. Test suites can be nested, so a suite can contain other suites.

❑   **Test runner** — A test runner, quite simply, runs tests. It is a component that facilitates the execution of a set of tests and the displaying of results to the user.

Example

As an example, let's build a test for the `createSnapshot()` method in the `snapshothelper.py` module. The following paths assume a Windows system, so adjust the directory paths as appropriate if you are on Unix or Linux. Here is what the file (`testsnapshothelper.py` in the Chapter 10 directory) looks like:

```python
import snapshothelper
import unittest
import os

class TestCreateSnapshot(unittest.TestCase):

    def setUp(self):
        import os
        os.chdir ('c:\\snapshots')

    def tearDown(self):
        os.system('del *.snp')

    def testpython25snap(self):
        # make a snapshot of the Python25 directory
        snapshothelper.createSnapshot('c:\\python25', 'python25snap.snp')
        assert 'python25snap.snp' in os.listdir(os.curdir), 'Snapshot not created!'

    def testprogramfilesdir(self):
        # make a snapshot of the Python25 directory
        snapshothelper.createSnapshot('c:\\program files', 'programfilessnap.snp')
        assert 'programfilessnap.snp' in os.listdir(os.curdir), 'Snapshot not
        created!'

if __name__ == '__main__':
    unittest.main()
```

The first thing the program does is import the modules it is going to need:

```python
import snapshothelper
import unittest
import os
```

Next, it initializes a class that is inherited from `unittest.TestCase`:

```python
class TestCreateSnapshot(unittest.TestCase):
```

Two special methods are the first methods in the class. The `setUp` method is run at the beginning of each test method in the class, and the `tearDown` method is run at the end of each test method:

```python
    def setUp(self):
        import os
        os.chdir ('c:\\snapshots')

    def tearDown(self):
        os.system('del *.snp')
```

Next are the test methods. Notice that each test methods begins with the word `test`. That's not just a naming convention — it tells the `TestCase` class that the method is a test method, to be run by the test runner.

Consider the first test method:

```
def testpython25snap(self):
    # make a snapshot of the Python25 directory
    snapshothelper.createSnapshot('c:\\python25', 'python25snap.snp')
    assert 'python25snap.snp' in os.listdir(os.curdir), 'Snapshot not created!'
```

Notice it simply contains code to exercise the function under test, and then an `assert` statement verifying that the function executed correctly.

The next test method is structured much the same — it is to test that you can create a snapshot for the program files directory, which has a space in the directory name:

```
def testprogramfilesdir(self):
    # make a snapshot of the Python25 directory
    snapshothelper.createSnapshot('c:\\program files', 'programfilessnap.snp')
    assert 'programfilessnap.snp' in os.listdir(os.curdir), 'Snapshot not created!'
```

Finally, the following lines of code, placed at the bottom of a test module, enable the tests to be run by simply executing the module:

```
if __name__ == '__main__':
    unittest.main()
```

Running the Tests

Go ahead and run the example by typing the following from a command prompt at the directory where you downloaded the files for Chapter 10: **python testsnapshothelper.py.**

You should see errors similar to the following:

```
EE
======================================================================
ERROR: testprogramfilesdir (__main__.TestCreateSnapshot)
----------------------------------------------------------------------
Traceback (most recent call last):
  File "testsnapshothelper.py", line 9, in setUp
    os.chdir ('c:\\snapshots')
WindowsError: [Error 2] The system cannot find the file specified: 'c:\\snapshots'

======================================================================
```

(continued)

(continued)

```
ERROR: testpython25snap (__main__.TestCreateSnapshot)
-------------------------------------------------------------------
Traceback (most recent call last):
  File "testsnapshothelper.py", line 9, in setUp
    os.chdir ('c:\\snapshots')
WindowsError: [Error 2] The system cannot find the file specified: 'c:\\snapshots'


-------------------------------------------------------------------
Ran 2 tests in 0.009s

FAILED (errors=2)
```

Ah, we forgot to create the `snapshots` directory. You can see how the output of errors or failing tests is formatted, to help you troubleshoot the results of the test run.

Create the `c:\snapshots` directory and run the test module again. You'll see the following:

```
Press [Enter] to continue...
.Press [Enter] to continue...
.
-------------------------------------------------------------------
Ran 2 tests in 18.081s

OK
```

Note that after each function you were prompted to press Enter. That's not a behavior of the test framework; the function itself does that. The output indicates that all the tests passed, and how long it took to run the tests.

doctest — a Compelling Alternative

Another option when building a framework for testing Python applications is `doctest`, a Python module that enables tests to be defined within `docstrings` as interactive sessions, and then run.

The best way to understand how it works is to look at a simple example, so let's do that now.

Example 1

This first example shows the simplest way of running a `doctest`, by embedding `docstrings` inside a function itself:

```
def printname(firstname, lastname):
    """Print firstname and lastname

    >>> printname("Jim", "Knowlton")
    Jim Knowlton
```

```
    >>> printname("John", "Doe")
    John Doe
    """
    print "%s %s" % (firstname, lastname)

def _test():
    import doctest
    doctest.testmod()

if __name__ == "__main__":
    _test()
```

This program defines a function `printname`, which takes a first name and a last name as parameters:

```
def printname(firstname, lastname):
```

This is followed by a comment (`docstring`) that shows the expected output of a test, written in the form of an interactive shell session:

```
"""Print firstname and lastname

>>> printname("Jim", "Knowlton")
Jim Knowlton
>>> printname("John", "Doe")
John Doe
"""
```

The next line is the actual functionality of the function, which prints the first name and last name, with a space in between:

```
print "%s %s" % (firstname, lastname)
```

The final block of code imports the `doctest` module and allows the `doctests` to be run when the module is executed:

```
def _test():
    import doctest
    doctest.testmod()

if __name__ == "__main__":
    _test()
```

Example 2

This example shows how tests can be defined in a simple text file, separate from the module itself, and run.

The `snapshottests.txt` text file (simply copied and pasted from an interactive session) is as follows:

```
>>> def printname(firstname, lastname):
...     print firstname + " " + lastname
...
>>> printname("Jim", "Knowlton")
Jim Knowlton
>>> printname("Bob")
Traceback (most recent call last):
  File "<stdin>", line 1, in <module>
TypeError: printname() takes exactly 2 arguments (1 given)
>>> printname("William", "Jennings", "Bryan")
Traceback (most recent call last):
  File "<stdin>", line 1, in <module>
TypeError: printname() takes exactly 2 arguments (3 given)
>>>
```

Now let's look at the `doctestexample2` module. It's very simple:

```
import doctest
doctest.testfile("snapshottests.txt")
```

As you can see, it is simply a matter of creating a text file from a Python interactive session and then creating a script that loads that text file (with the help of the `testfile()` function).

If the module is run from the command line with a `-v` option (for verbose), it generates the following output:

```
Trying:
    def printname(firstname, lastname):
        print firstname + " " + lastname
Expecting nothing
ok
Trying:
    printname("Jim", "Knowlton")
Expecting:
    Jim Knowlton
ok
Trying:
    printname("Bob")
Expecting:
    Traceback (most recent call last):
      File "<stdin>", line 1, in <module>
    TypeError: printname() takes exactly 2 arguments (1 given)
ok
Trying:
    printname("William", "Jennings", "Bryan")
```

```
Expecting:
    Traceback (most recent call last):
      File "<stdin>", line 1, in <module>
    TypeError: printname() takes exactly 2 arguments (3 given)
ok
1 items passed all tests:
   4 tests in snapshottests.txt
4 tests in 1 items.
4 passed and 0 failed.
Test passed.
```

Summary

This chapter wasn't about writing code — it was about making code *right*. This can often be the most critical phase of software development, where "thinking like the customer" enables robust tests to be developed, and troubleshooting skills can facilitate solving thorny problems. Python provides some great tools to enable developers to effectively perfect their code.

This chapter covered the following main topics:

- ❏ The Python debugger, including the following:
  - ❏ Importing the pdb module directly through the Python interactive interpreter
  - ❏ Accessing the debugger through the IDLE
- ❏ Python test frameworks, including the following:
  - ❏ unittest (PyTest)
  - ❏ doctest

Final Remarks

If you've made it all the way through this book, congratulations. You now know how to access files, work with databases, communicate via Internet protocols, access operating system resources, and more — all from a popular, free, open-source, mature, fun programming language. Your work life — and your life in general — may never be the same.

Where to Go From Here — Resources That Can Help

As indicated throughout the preceding chapters, the purpose of this book has been to provide you with the tools you need to be productive with Python, and to avoid areas that might have less universal appeal. However, as you develop your knowledge and use of Python, you will no doubt want to delve into deeper waters.

This appendix suggests some resources I have found to be immensely useful.

Books

❑   *Learning Python, Third Edition,* by Mark Lutz (O'Reilly, 2007) — This is a great introductory overview of the Python language itself. It doesn't delve deeply into all the different Python modules, but rather focuses on the language. As such, it's a good companion volume to this book.

❑   *Python Cookbook,* by Alex Martelli, Anna Ravenscroft, and David Ascher (O'Reilly, 2005) — This is an excellent collection of "recipes" for accomplishing different tasks in Python. Each chapter is accompanied by an introductory section.

❑   *Core Python, Second Edition,* by Wesley Chun (Prentice Hall, 2006) — This is another great book that both provides introductory material and delves more deeply into areas such as object-oriented development with Python.

❏ *Beginning Python (Programmer to Programmer)*, by Peter C. Norton, Alex Samuel, Dave Aitel, and Eric Foster-Johnson (Wrox, 2005) — This volume strikes just the right balance between deep coverage of the Python language and offering real-world scenarios demonstrating how you can apply the concepts. If you don't opt for *Core Python,* this is a good addition for your bookshelf.

❏ *Beginning Python: From Novice to Professional*, by Magnus Lie Hetland (Apress, 2005) — This book provides a solid introduction to the language. Originally titled *Practical Python*, this book has been around for awhile and has undergone some good revisions.

❏ *Dive into Python*, by Mark Pilgrim (Apress, 2004) — This is a unique introduction to Python that teaches Python by beginning with the code itself, rather than using text to introduce a concept and then illustrate it with code.

❏ *Professional Python Frameworks: Web 2.0 Programming with Django and Turbogears (Programmer to Programmer)* by Dana Moore, Raymond Budd, and William Wright (Wrox, 2007) — This is a great book that introduces the popular Django and Turbogears frameworks, which are based on Python code. This book is a must if you want to use these frameworks to do Python-based web development.

Websites and Blogs

❏ You are likely to find the following sites useful: `www.python.org` — The official Python website.

❏ `wiki.python.org/moin` — The Python wiki. This is a Great place to learn about Python from the source.

❏ `planet.python.org` — The official Python blog, it has references to dozens of other Python blogs, and contributions from many experts.

❏ `about.python.com` — About.com's Python portal. It contains a lot of great information, reference material, and a blog.

These are the blogs I read regularly:

❏ `www.artima.com/weblogs/index.jsp?blogger=guido` — Guido Van Rossum's blog. Guido, as the creator of Python and "Benevolent Dictator for Life," is obviously a must-read for all Pythonistas.

❏ `agiletesting.blogspot.com` — Grig Gheorghiu's blog, which is especially focused on agile testing with Python.

❏ `blog.ianbicking.org` — Ian Bicking's blog on agile development with Python.

❏ `ivory.idyll.org/blog` — "Daily Life in an Ivory Basement," the blog of Titus Brown.

Installing Supplemental Programs

This appendix contains the instructions for installing MySQL, to support the database application in Chapter 5, and Win32All, to support some of the Python Windows integration described in Chapter 9.

Installing MySQL

MySQL is an open-source database server very popular in open-source software development. The following instructions will guide you through the install. However, for the most current information, go to the MySQL website at `http://www.mysql.org`.

Downloading the MySQL Community Server

In a web browser, navigate to `http://dev.mysql.com/downloads`. You will see a screen like the one shown in Figure B-1.

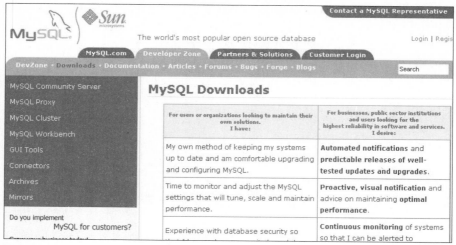

Figure B-1

Click the MySQL Community Server link on the sidebar on the left. After you are taken to the next page, you can scroll down to see a list of operating systems, as shown in Figure B-2.

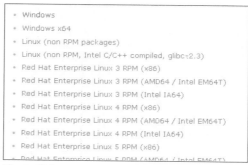

Figure B-2

Click the operating system on which you want to install (these instructions assume you are installing on Windows).

After doing that, you will be taken to a downloads screen, as shown in Figure B-3.

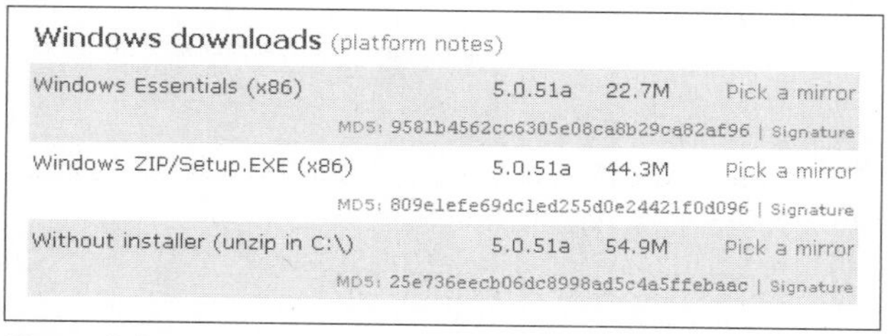

Figure B-3

Scroll down to the bottom of the next page, and click the link "No thanks, just take me to the downloads!"

You will be taken to a page with a list of locations from which you can download. After clicking the ftp link next to a location close to you, you'll see the Security Warning dialog shown in Figure B-4.

Figure B-4

Click Run.

Running the Install

After the download completes, the Welcome screen of the Setup Wizard will appear, as shown in Figure B-5.

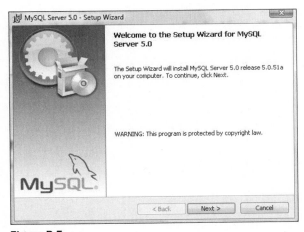

Figure B-5

Click Next. Figure B-6 shows the Setup Type dialog that will appear, from which you can select the appropriate install type.

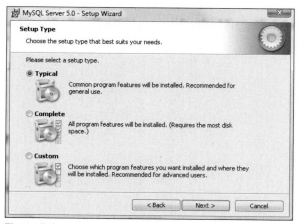

Figure B-6

For the purposes of this book, it's perfectly adequate to perform a "typical" install, so click Next.

You'll be presented with the install confirmation screen, shown in Figure B-7.

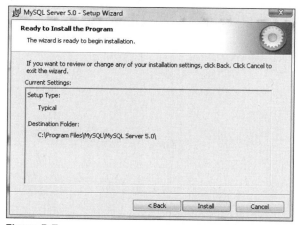

Figure B-7

Click Install to begin the install. When the install is completed, you'll see the Wizard Completed dialog shown in Figure B-8.

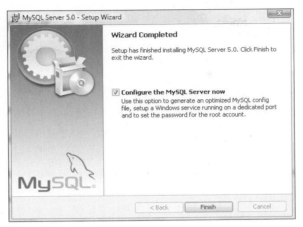

Figure B-8

Click Finish to configure the MySQL server.

Configuring the MySQL Server

Figure B-9 shows the first page of the Configuration Wizard that appears after the install is completed.

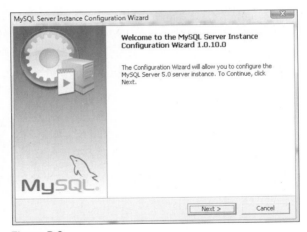

Figure B-9

Click Next. Figure B-10 shows the dialog that appears, from which you can pick a configuration type.

Figure B-10

For the purposes of this book, a standard configuration is sufficient, so click the Standard Configuration radio button and click Next.

In the dialog that appears next, shown in Figure B-11, you can install MySQL as a Windows service and include the MySQL bin directory in the Windows path. Make sure both are checked and click Next.

Figure B-11

You'll then see the dialog shown in Figure B-12, which contains some security options.

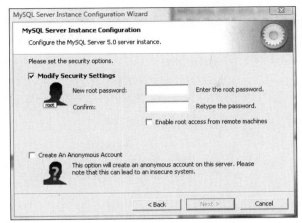

Figure B-12

As shown in Figure B-12, enter a root password and click Next. The dialog shown in Figure B-13 will appear.

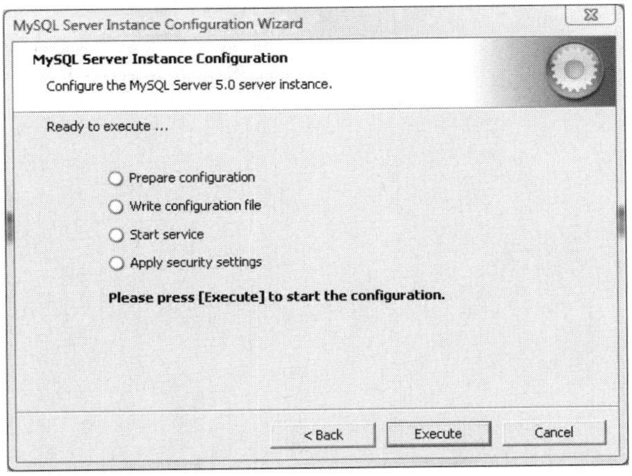

Figure B-13

Click Execute to run the configuration.

When the configuration is finished, click Exit to close the Configuration Wizard. MySQL is now installed and configured.

Installing Win32All

Win32All is a collection of add-ons and APIs that enable a Python developer to interact with Windows.

Downloading the Win32All Package

> Win32All requires that Python (minimum version: 2.2) already be installed on a
> Windows system.

In a web browser, navigate to `http://sourceforge.net/projects/pywin32/`. You will see
the Python for Windows Extensions window shown in Figure B-14.

Figure B-14

Click the Download the Python for Windows Extensions link. Scroll down the page to the section that is
shown in Figure B-15.

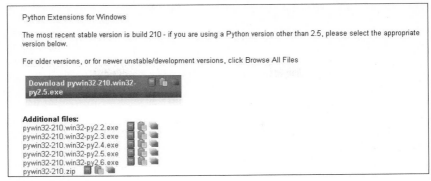

Figure B-15

Notice that downloads are available for versions of Python from 2.2 through 2.6. Click the appropriate link for the version of Python you have installed and you'll get a prompt to download the file (assuming the security set for your browser allows you to download files), as shown in Figure B-16.

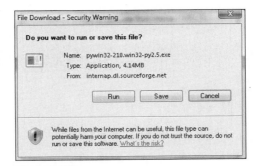

Figure B-16

Click Run.

Running the Install

After the file downloads, the install will start and the dialog shown in Figure B-17 will appear.

Figure B-17

Click Next. As shown in Figure B-18, you'll be prompted with the location of your version of Python, which the install will locate in the Windows Registry.

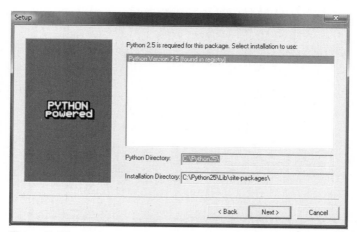

Figure B-18

Click Next. Figure B-19 shows the confirmation dialog that will appear.

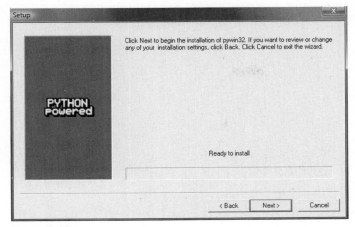

Figure B-19

Click Next to begin the install. When the install is finished, the dialog shown in Figure B-20 will appear, indicating the log of the successful install.

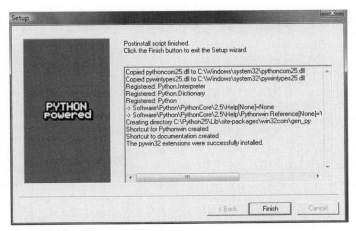

Figure B-20

Click Finish to exit the install.

Win32All is now installed.

Index